Pick of Punch

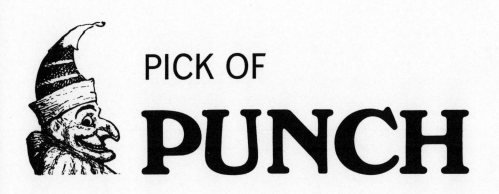

PICK OF

PUNCH

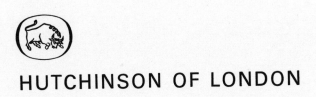

HUTCHINSON OF LONDON

A Punch book, published by
Hutchinson & Co. *(Publishers)* Ltd.
3 Fitzroy Square, London, W.1

London   Melbourne   Sydney   Auckland
Wellington   Johannesburg   Cape Town
and agencies throughout the world

© 1973 by Punch Publications Limited
ALL RIGHTS RESERVED
Printed in Great Britain by
George Pulman & Sons Ltd.
ISBN 0 09 118540 8

Contents

Introduction

The problem, with each Pick of Punch, is how to provide a reasonably accurate reflection of all the effort which goes into producing a magazine which appears every week. So much of our comment —particularly on political affairs—dates very quickly and does not really belong in an annual anthology, especially one which is read all over the world. Besides, I'm not at all sure that the many thousands of readers who buy these volumes every year are obsessed by politics—let alone the grievances, jealousies, and vendettas of people in journalism, public relations, and advertising. There *is* a world outside Westminster and Fleet Street. So although you will find political comment in this "Pick"—notably a selection of Trog's cartoons—my chief aim in choosing the material has been to make you laugh and, at the same time, to offer sharp, irreverent observation on the changing social scene.

I realise that you may find some of the things in this book unfunny: one of the first lessons one learns in this business is that humour is a matter of individual taste, and that an article or cartoon which makes one man laugh will probably make another man very angry. But I hope you will agree that, on balance, the Pick of Punch represents an entertaining—and, indeed, unique—record of some of the year's more interesting events. Some of our earlier volumes have become collector's items and, looking at them again, I don't find it difficult to see why. They certainly give me much personal pleasure: it's so much easier to keep today's issues in perspective (and learn to live with them) if you can take a detached view of some of the major topics of the past.

WILLIAM DAVIS

What's a Nice Guy Like You Doing in a Bunker Like This?

by AL CAPP

Old anti-Nazi movies on TV re-runs are now so popular that a new one, starring Alec Guinness as Hitler, is in production, and several others are scheduled. The reason we are all so nostalgic about the Nazis, is that, since then, we really haven't had anyone to hate.

There is so much love and understanding around now that anyone who can pronounce schizophrenic (and an alarming number of us can) can explain why Charles Manson needs love more than maximum security.

You could once rely on an eruption of blind, unreasoning hate in the USA, at any rate, during any Presidential campaign. What little there was of it, in this one, went, when George Wallace was shot. We could enjoy hating Wallace while the little man was strutting and snarling around the country sneering at "pointey-headed intellectuals" but we were transformed into fellow human beings at the sight of him, fallen and bleeding, and later gaunt and gallant, in his wheelchair. As for his assassin there never was, nor I predict, will there be, any genuine hate for him. We all understand that he was a lonely lad, who didn't mean to hurt anyone, but only to beg for affection.

Liberals were prepared to hate Richard Nixon for his campaign tactics, but that all went for nothing, because he didn't bother to campaign. On the other hand no conservative hates George McGovern any more than a plain woman hates an even plainer one who makes her look good.

Even General Amin has been unable to provoke any respectable amount of hatred in the USA. We are so understanding about that sort of thing we understand how reasonable it is for a black to be a racist since they, themselves were, so long, victims of racism.

Jane Fonda, it might seem, should have earned the pure unadulterated hate that kept Tokyo Rose out of our physical reach, but even those Americans who are baffled at Jane's message that it is beastly for non-Communists to fight back, are understanding enough to defend her right to appear on our TV networks, to denounce the lack of freedom of expression on our TV networks, and to charge, at American Army combat training camps, that the American Army is prone to violence.

Even though Teddy Kennedy is the most admired spokesman for the American Party that most heartily opposes special privilege for the rich and powerful, he has our understanding, and, if to prove that he has it, we must give him the Presidency in '76, millions of us are not going to be hateful enough to deprive him of it.

Once the movies gave us someone to hate; the crooks, the seducers of innocents, the snobs who considered themselves above average citizens. They've taken all that away from us. The biggest hits of the last couple of years were *Easy Rider* and *The Godfather*. In *Easy Rider* a couple of young dope-peddlers used their profits to embark on a cross-country joyride, seducing local innocents, and jeering at louts who worked for a living.

The film ended when they both had their heads blown off as they were passing the car of a couple of average citizens, with the average reaction to hippies, but who, luckily, had guns on them at the time. I consider it a happy ending bringing back at last, the custom of giving the bad guys what they deserved, and I was stunned to discover that everyone else considered them good guys, and the ending a tragic one.

The Godfather was an unashamedly sentimental portrait of a throat-cutter and thief, who brought his children up to be throat-cutters and thieves, and whose death made audiences weep, instead of cheer, as they would have in another time, before understanding had made social workers of us all.

For a while, we, in America, were given someone to hate, ourselves. This was taught us by our children and minorities and for years we grovelled in it, moaning "What have we done wrong?" and "It's up to you, from the campuses and the ghettoes, to create a world we were too blind, selfish and stupid to create!" until it dawned on us that our young could be pretty damned hateful themselves and that the minorities were getting the majority of our taxes.

Only the Nazis are left for us to hate, and that's why we all so love old

"Look, Sam, I know you are not going to believe this—it's some people enquiring about a set!"

"Don't you think you're slightly overdoing your experiments on that poor dog?"

Nazi movies. They were not only bestial to their enemies, but to each other, of lower rank. It was nothing for a Nazi officer to personally shoot dead an underling who had, even for a moment, been deceived by a spy he had captured and brought in. And they didn't want their captives to talk. Not right away. Not until they had a chance to use "their ways". Those ways of theirs were so hideous they were never shown. All we heard were the screams from behind closed doors, which irritated the officer since, at the time, he was rambling on about the quality of the champagne in the chateau, and regretting that the victim's mother wouldn't join him in a toast to the Fuehrer.

Our hate for the character men who played Nazis was so deep and enduring none of them ever got work again, once the vogue was over. Except George Sanders, the most hateful of them all, and that was because he was really a member of the British Secret Service.

But if charmers like Guinness play Hitler, we may, I'm afraid, begin to understand them, and once that happens we're lost. Take it from one who lives in a country that's been through it; the beginning of understanding is the end of hate. And a world without healthy, invigorating, blood-rousing hate, is a turgid and passionless future to look forward to. Yet there may be a glimmer of hope.

On BBC the other night, a sub-human gunman, thief and escaped convict took over and terrorised the home of his clean-living hard-working brother, his motherly sister-in-law and their sweet little daughter. When it was over, you had been made to love the gunman, and detest the wholesome little family.

It may be that hate is not dead, but in good health and working for the BBC. The same old hate, but directed at something new—at everything that isn't hateful.

Brats Precocious

by MIKE WILLIAMS

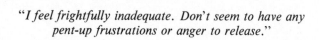

"I feel frightfully inadequate. Don't seem to have any pent-up frustrations or anger to release."

"I realise this probably indicates a certain lack of fundamental maturity but I actually prefer baby talk."

"I often wonder what we'd do without television."

"Shouldn't we get someone in to do that sort of thing, Mother?"

The Truth Shall Make You Free!

cries KEITH WATERHOUSE

The Kosycot Happiness Through Effort, Solidarity And Never Owing Nobody For Nothink Always Paid Cash On The Nail It Has Been Our One Rule In Life family collective voluntarily and unanimously gave up its Sunday lie-in recently in order to hold a spontaneous meeting for the purposes of self-criticism and to demonstrate solidarity against the running dogs of imperialism at No 43 next door what has the radio blaring out at all hours, as for their son Barry he is nothink but a jackal of the reactionary capitalist system and a cheeky young devil, why don't they make him get his hair cut.

Present at this voluntary assembly were Our Dad, Our Mum, Our Gran, Our Noreen, Our Noreen's husband Barry, Young Kevin, and Mr. Nightingale what was present in an honorary capacity being as how him and Our Dad always have a couple of pints at The Crooked Billet of a Sunday dinner-time, it is invariably the Crooked Billet these days, have given up The Green Man completely. Landlord does not properly understand the nature of the class struggle also beer is like dishwater.

Our Dad rose at 10.30 a.m. and received a standing ovation. The family collective passed a unanimous and spontaneous resolution that Young Kevin should give over chucking bits of toast.

Our Dad said that he had only this to say, everythink was blooming marvellous, in fact it was all a very good thing, what the State had done for the common man. Under the corrupt filthy swinish Tory capitalist system, mark you he was going back a bit now, he (Our Dad) had been nothink but a lousy stinking bus conductor, twenty-two quid a week, overtime if you was lucky, whereas since the elimination of economic exploitation and what with Old Jack retiring through his leg, he had now risen to be an Inspector on the Astounding Joy Through Satisfaction Public Transport Facility, what used to be the old London Transport.

He was earning good money and was pleased to report that by applying true revolutionary principles and cutting down on fags, the family collective had now reached its target of sixty-four quid for new telly, Mr. Nightingale knew where he could get colour set for that price, ask no questions get no lies told. The clothing club norm had also been reached so no problem about school blazer for Young Kevin, as for holiday at the Mao Tse-Tung Hotel on the Costa Brava it was definitely fixed, so don't nobody start changing their minds and wanting to go to the Spirit of the People caravan site at Southend, forty quid for the week and take your own bleeding food, we (the family collective) should cocoa.

However, Our Dad was forced to pass the remark that while the family collective was keeping up to scratch as regards building for socialism through diligence and frugality, somebody was still putting toffee papers down the lav. He did not blame Our Gran: the silly old twat was a victim of the political oppression of the peasants back in the old days and could no more grasp the Marxist philosophy of dialectical materialism than pigs could fly.

All Our Dad was asking for was just that bit of give and take. If the family collective played fair by him, he would play fair by the family collective. If, on the other hand, the family collective wanted to do things the hard way, there was always the Wellbeing Of The Masses Old People's Home for them what refused to toe the line, same as Our Noreen's husband Barry, if he had been told not to lean his bicycle against the sideboard once he had been told a million times, it was about time him and

Noreen got a flat of their own. Long live the People's Revolution.

Our Mam, in proposing a toast to the Leader of the People's Democracy without whose inspiration the struggle of the masses would have been in vain, said that Our Dad was a paper tiger. He was always wittering. Nobody was perfect and she herself had made errors and in future would strive to correct her mistaken ideas. Give you an example: contrary to the teachings of the Strength Through Nourishment Cut Out And Keep Recipe Page in the People's Daily, Our Mam had been over-whisking her egg whites, result being that the cheese souffle had been coming out all runny. By applying the three main rules of socialist discipline, she would see that this did not happen again.

However, Our Dad should take a look in the mirror and correct his own tendency towards negativism before going on about other people's toffee papers and bicycles. If he had built a bike shed back in the corrupt era of two thousand years of feudalism, same as what he always said he was going to do, he would have no need to be moaning on about scratches on the sideboard during the present enlightened dawning of a true communist system.

Also, it was all very well putting money on one side for colour tellies what had fallen off of the back of a lorry, but Our Mam could not manage on the housekeeping. Due to the fact that consumer goods were no longer monopolised by a privileged class but were available to the masses, prices had gone up somethink shocking. Also, if the wife of the enemy of progress and toady of the bourgeoisie at No. 43 could have three new coats a year, there was no reason why Our Mam should not have a new dress once in a blue moon. May the People's Desire to Achieve Stability by Applying Marxist Thinking Be Quickly Realised.

Resolved: to pop down to the Doves Of Everlasting Peace Cut-Price Shop and see what they are asking for them flowered poplin pinafore dresses what they have in the window.

Our Gran, after declaring that the high tide of social transformation would soon sweep over the whole country, admitted that she had been guilty of revisionist tendencies. She had fancied Bakewell Tart in the 3.30 at Kempton Park, contrary to the teachings of Our Dad which were that he had seen better horses being carted into the People's Sausage Factory. She now wished to confess her recidivism and in future would back nothink but the favourite. Only thus could the proletariat be triumphant in its ceaseless struggle towards an ideological society. On the other hand, Our Gran's back was playing her up somethink awful. She could not sleep and had got this stabbing pain that started in her hands and went all up her arms and round her shoulders, she blamed that pork chop she had for her tea last night, it was all gristle. A

"Do you want me to read to you this morning, Mrs. Simpson?"

"Do you mind if I shelter from the rain? I am waiting for a friend."

thousand years of peace to the People's Democracy.

Resolved: to get some more of that liniment.

Our Noreen's husband Barry, in suggesting that the family collective should be even more vigilant in its efforts to avoid the corrosive influence of so called Liberalism, asked Our Dad if he was dropping the hint that he should leave the bike out in the back garden in future. If so, he could tell Our Dad for nothink that the reactionary elements and enemies of the people at No. 43 would have it away before you could say Mao Tse-Tung. He had said nothing before as he did not want to cause trouble, but if you asked him anythink Our Dad did not know the first

thing about the correct handling of contradictions among the working-class cadres, in fact he did not know his arse from his elbow. Goodwill towards the Annual National Congress of the Cultural Committee of the Communist Party, and stuff the whole lot of you.

Resolved: that our Noreen's husband Barry gets his name down for a worker's flat sharpish.

It being opened time, the meeting adjourned after singing the *Red Flag* and separating Our Dad and our Noreen's husband Barry in the interests of greater understanding.

Long live the Kosycot family collective.

Down with the running jackals at No. 43.

If you're Irish—what are you doing about it?

"Well, most of us in England," says Seamus MAHOOD, "feeling guilty about our 'bombing bigots' image, are trying to become indistinguishable from your average humane, moderate, apathetic Englishman."

"Sean, Patraig, Eamonn, I now rechristen you Edward, Harold, Jeremy . . ."

*" Your feelings about recent events do you credit, Mr. McShany. And what better way to remove that conscience-stricken feeling than by buying a **British** car?"*

"Paddy is finding it all a bit of a strain—he still hasn't got over the shock of celebrating St. Patrick's Day sotto voce!"

"Rooney, Ryan, MacNally and Kelly will continue to do the blasting but I've taken on Fetherstonhaugh here to hold the key to the gelly store."

"I thought you said Mr. Kelly wanted to remain incognito"

"I suppose it's too much to expect decent leadership back home, when you consider that the crème de la crème of the nation is here in Camden Town."

"Our distinguished prosecutor here has made a very strong case against the Irish. I now call the first witness for the defence!"

R.I.P.

MICHAEL McMURPHY
1905-1973

"I AM NOT NOW, AND NEVER HAVE BEEN, A MEMBER OF THE I.R.A. OR THE U.D.A. OR THE REST OF THAT ILK"

"I still say they all protest too much."

BEFORE   AFTER

How to Slim

by TERRY JONES
of Monty Python's Flying Circus

Are you *hideously* and *repulsively* FAT? Eurrrrrrgh! How HORRIBLE! I'm certainly glad *I* don't know you! In fact I'm surprised you weren't too embarrassed and ashamed to walk down the street to buy this magazine. I expect when you did everyone was pointing at you behind your back and saying: "Isn't he FAT!" and "Why doesn't he get SLIM?" and "I wouldn't like him to sit/lie/jump up and down on *me*!" No wonder you're reading this page! Well, let me tell you, you are doing EXACTLY THE RIGHT THING. So keep reading. You have just taken the first step towards getting slim, because this whole article is designed to tell you HOW TO SLIM (see title).

For too long now HOW TO SLIM has been a closely guarded secret jealously kept by those who *are* slim from those who are fat and nasty. Well, at last, I am prepared to divulge the secret to you—NO MATTER HOW FAT YOU ARE! All you need to do is keep reading this article, and the SECRET will be yours. Once in possession of THE SECRET, all you have to do is become slim, and the whole world of sexual promiscuity will open up in front of you. So don't stop reading now! You are just about to gain possession of THE SECRET.

In fact it's on the very next line—so only a few more words of drivel and the SECRET is yours! Here it is (When I said "the next line" I didn't mean it absolutely literally. I'm sorry if I misled anyone, but please don't start writing in and complaining, because it's not worth it. You won't be pointing out to me anything I didn't already know, and in any case nobody likes clever dicks—especially fat ones.) Anyway you are just about to become the proud possessor of THE SECRET of HOW TO SLIM. (This time it certainly *is* on the next line.)

There is one sure way HOW TO SLIM. *DON'T EAT ANYTHING AT ALL!* That way all your hideous excess fat falls off almost overnight. *I know*, I have DONE it!

Once you have grasped this fundamental principle of How To Slim, you are in possession of THE SECRET, and now you no longer need to ask the question "How To Slim?" The question you need to ask is: "How Not To Eat Anything At All?" This is more difficult. I won't make any bones about it. It is a *Problem*. But don't panic! I have the answer, because I have *done* it. I lost 2 stones in 3 weeks, simply by not eating anything at all . . . well I *did* have a curry on the third day, but that's not the point. The point is How Did *I* Not Eat Anything at All?

What did I do? Well the answer is: I didn't do anything. My wife did. She left me.

Now since (a) I like good food and (b) company and (c) she is a better cook than I am and (d) I was no longer eligible for wife-swapping discussion-groups, I decided to eat nothing at all for two days.

Now, if you weigh yourself last thing at night and first thing in the morning, you will find that just by lying asleep you have lost 2 lbs. If you don't eat the next day you lose another

18

2 lbs, so that by the evening you will be 4 lbs lighter and 6 lbs lighter by the next morning. So you can lose 6 lbs in two days simply by Not Eating Anything At All!

So the fundamental principle of How Not To Eat Anything At All is: Get Your Wife To Leave You. This is your Key to How To Slim.

The next question is clear: How To Get Your Wife To Leave You? Well this is not at all as difficult as you may imagine. In fact you may be pleasantly surprised at how easy it is. Don't forget you already have a considerable advantage, being so hideously and repulsively fat, Eurrrrrrgh! Your wife will probably be only too glad to go off and find some slim-hipped 18-year-old youth who's actually *read* Buckminster Fuller.

Of course, there are two possible snags: (a) she may prefer seedy, middle-aged, fat men or (b) she may herself be seedy, middle-aged and fat and unlikely to pick up anyone who's even read *Dr. Zhivago*. In the case of (a) you seem to have the best of all possible worlds and shouldn't be reading this article. In the case of (b) this is quite some problem, and, in fact, you may end up having to leave *her*, which is a terrible business, involving booking hotel rooms, finding somewhere else to live, moving your things out, and really I can't recommend it AT ALL. No, it's much better if you can get *her* to leave *you*.

There are two general methods of Getting Your Wife To Leave You: either brute force or persuasion. The first method is certainly quick and effective, but has snags. If, for example, your wife puts up particularly strong resistance, it's going to be *you* who has to do all the clearing-up afterwards, and I can tell you it's no fun trying to fix broken furniture or getting bloodstains out of the Axminster without the gentle hand of a help-mate. There is also the possibility of legal action—even criminal proceedings—which, while it might certainly take off a few pounds, might also interfere with your enjoyment of the SEXUAL PROMISCUITY which Slimness will make yours. So the only method I can really whole-heartedly recommend is Persuasion. It's legal, inexpensive and kind to the hands.

So the question How To Slim has now been greatly simplified. All you need to know is: How To Get Your Wife To Want To Leave You? This one's a piece of cake. Don't forget you already have a headstart being so HIDEOUSLY and REPULSIVELY Obese. All you have to do is cultivate this innate unattractiveness.

For instance, pay a little more attention to those unpleasant personal habits. Try picking in between your toes on *her* side of the bed. Use Trex instead of Brylcream. Or simply start shaving your legs. Another good ploy is to make your wife feel inadequate. Start getting up a couple of hours before you go to work and whip round the house with a duster, hoover the carpets and put the supper on for the evening, so that by the time she comes down, looking awful and coughing from her first fag of the day, you're all bright and alert, have done all the housework and are just off for a full day at the office/mortuary/limb-fitting centre or wherever.

Or how about simply making her life with you a misery? You could start by trying to recreate *Die Fledermaus* in soft toys, or crazy-paving the sitting-room or ordering a new gas stove or any of a 1001 things which you will find in my book *How To Get Your Wife To Want To Leave You And Your Money Back* by a Well-Known Brand of Typewriter Ribbon.

"Gerald, think of the children."

19

Well! Now you've got rid of her. The door has slammed. The note is on the table. The hot-pot is in the fridge. God's in his heaven and the Dirty Fido's in her work basket where you left it. Suddenly you don't feel like eating any more. You stop. Next day . . . 6 lbs lighter! "Impossible" I hear you mutter into your avocado vinaigrette? Let me repeat: I have DONE IT!

Yet one question remains. The mysteries of slimness that have eluded you for so many painfully humiliating years are at last made clear to you (for no other cost than the price of this magazine*) and yet, you will be saying—there still remains the one vital question: How To *Stay* Slim? Well you will probably be not at all surprised to hear that I have the answer for this too, and—AT NO EXTRA COST**—I am prepared to divulge all.

This is me divulging it . . . The point *is:* I like eating food. I also like having sex. And this is the crux. You will soon discover, now that your HIDEOUS and REPULSIVE obesity no longer scars the landscape, that the glittering and spangly world of *Sexual Promiscuity* has opened up before you. You will suddenly discover that maidens are no longer less forward than they used to be. You will discover that the days are not passed forever when a gentle rose will blush to see a manly shape. You will discover that what had been missing was the shape, and

that now you are in proud repossession of IT. Sexual pleasure is the great consolation of the Slim.

Of course, you might decide that you enjoy eating food more than having sex, in which case, my sincere advice is that you eat as much as you possibly can until the end of your life without being ill. But if, like me, you find it hard to choose between the two, or preferably—would rather have both—one after the other—then my advice is: on the one hand don't have so much sex that you can't eat, and, on the other, don't eat so much food that people no longer want you to sit/lie/jump up and down on them in the way that is currently fashionable with us humans.

I would like to point out that this article is written entirely free of charge, and donated to this publication in the sincere hope that it may improve the lot of my fellow men. Ladies reading this article are reminded that the author has probably only another 30 years or so left in which to sit/lie/jump up and down and they should contact him without delay.

Do not believe rumours that my wife has returned.

My waist is *still* only 30 inches!

*Donations are, however, always welcome.

**The author is always open to contributions NO MATTER HOW SLIM.

"We're thinking of leaving home, dear."

The Body as Medium of Expression

Has talking with words made us forget how to talk with our body movements? asks the ICA in its current show. Nonsense! Here's how we do it . . .

◄By crossing his hands in opposite directions and staring firmly through dark glasses at a dark room, this man's body is clearly trying to tell us something. It is saying: "On the one hand, on the other hand, I completely agree but I reserve the option to disagree, this has never been our policy". It is a frank and sincere body with overtones of doubletalk.

By running in his vest and underpants in a public place, this man is telling us via his body that he does not give two hoots for public opinion. I may have failed, it says, but it's nothing to do with you. From the style it is apparent that the man is not a natural runner and would have to practise very hard to be any good at all. Why is he running, then? Perhaps he has missed the bus. ►

◄The baton—a symbol of authority. The whole attitude of the body is a threat: "If you do not do what I say, I shall beat you", while the smile is a reward "If you do what I say, I shall be pleased, though I shall probably beat you anyway". A man in command, whoever he is. A sea captain perhaps?

A happy man, one with a rollicking sense of humour, almost certainly a great addict of *Punch*. But are things so simple? Look at the hands. They seem to be breaking bread. Look closer, at the way he clutches the bread, the way the thumbs are firmly stuck in the dough. What he is actually doing is grimly keeping the two halves of the loaf apart, almost as if he is afraid they will leap on each other and make wholemeal love. There is a conflict between the puritan and the sensualist somewhere here. ►

An interesting pair of bodies here. Both men are obviously in the same line of business (part of big international organisations, judging from the uniform) but note the difference in attitude. The man on the left makes timid gestures with his right hand (and only two fingers at that), puts his left hand across himself defensively and wears a half-smile, half-frown on his face. No sign of ambition or drive here, whereas the man on the right, with no need to bolster his confidence by means of grandiloquent costume, has a strong open face and presents the full palm of the hand to his audience. It's safe to say that the former will never rise high in his firm; the latter must be a man of great stature and importance.

"Is this bush taken?"

ffull ffrontal ffolkes

"She's brilliant but she would be even better with a bat."

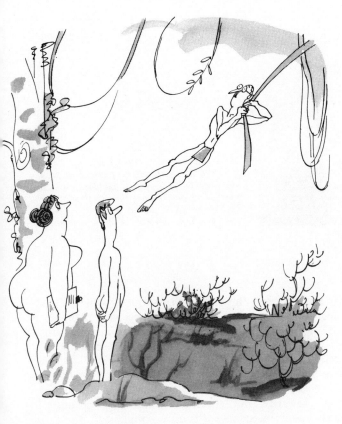

"We make an exception of Mr. Turnbull. He had
a rather unfortunate accident last year."

"Now, Miss Hartley, I'm sure we're not
as busy as all that!"

"Why, Miss Carstairs, without your
glasses you're **beautiful**!"

". . . a shudder went through his being as he watched
her bosom heave under the thick polo-necked sweater
peeping above the heavy folds of her anorak."

Great Summers: PETER USTINOV

Actor, playwright, novelist, mimic, wit, PETER USTINOV is a fascinating crowd of people. He lives in Switzerland, London, Paris and most other places from time to time and says he likes to go on talking because he finds out what he thinks that way. Some days he just sits.

Summer has, for me, the element of sadness which colours all high points in existence. Just as a rare moment of personal triumph is tinged by a dawning sense of the barrenness of life suddenly deprived of a particular ambition, now fulfilled, so summer becomes too soon, almost at its very inception, a drift into autumn, the passing of a prime. Autumn has its own beauties once it is accepted—in fact, it is often far lovelier than summer, but this only once it is present, just as an acceptance of old age can produce the most exquisite rewards, but the first white hair sprouts in summer, and is given especial attention because it is unseasonal.

It is hard, almost impossible to single out a summer as being particularly great, for the summers of extreme youth are recollected by details such as the triangular tube of Walls's water ice, in which the discreet taste of cardboard in the last liquid drops gave a peculiar and delicious tang to the flavour of lime, or by all the devious strategies to avoid catching a cricket ball as it hurtled unswervingly in the direction of this unwilling player. I remember clearly shouting "Butter-fingers" myself one second before I dropped the ball, thereby depriving others of that pleasure.

But there is no consistency in these memories. They are just individual stones of a lost mosaic. Far from schooldays being the happiest time of life, I don't believe I actually enjoyed a summer to the full until I was my own master, and no longer a timorous victim of a morbid fear of wasps, dogs and other forms of life to which I groundlessly attributed an inherent malevolence.

It was probably a moment of utter folly relatively late in life which led to my most intoxicating discovery, that of the therapeutic effect of the sea, not as shallows filled with squealing children and peeling nymphs, but as a vast and somnolent expanse of history. Let me explain myself. Sometime in the late fifties I was invited to a cocktail party aboard a boat in Cannes harbour. Marinas had not yet come into existence, but smart seaports like Cannes had already developed into libraries of boats, nestling together and showing tantalizing evidence of the life aboard. Old millionaires who never put to sea sat in Ruritanian naval uniforms drinking dry Martinis, while ladies in less than ample pants spent their time arranging bouquets of flowers or pretending to, followed hither and thither by tiny maritime dogs. The Rolls-Royce and Ferraris with Monegasque or even more exotic plates waited patiently on the mole, to take their charges back to hotel or villa after a hard day's sailing in the harbour.

I plunged into this unpromising atmosphere and found my sea-legs with difficulty, standing there in a summer-weight lounge suit but with bare feet in order not to damage the deck, I drank the Martinis I was given, and then no longer recollect precisely what occurred; whether it was an excess of an inhabitual beverage in the heat or whether I experienced a profane vision on a road to Damascus made to my measure, the fact remains that before I left the party I had both purchased the boat and hired the Captain. It was a crazy decision I have never regretted.

Since my family fortune (long since lost and by no means recovered) was made in Siberia, yes, in the salt-mines, this urge towards the sea may be the result of an atavistic instinct common to all Russians to replace the monotony of the steppes for at least a new monotony, that of the unsuspected ocean. Whatever the truth of this, I now protect my deck with a surly vigilance, and the shedding of the shoes is as stringent a ritual as in any mosque.

I remember a British Admiral coming aboard and complimenting the Captain on the excellent condition of the deck. "What do you use on it?" barked the visitor, "sand-paper?" "No, senor, El Omo," replied the Captain, which proves, at least, that we live with the times on occasion, except that whenever I could still afford to put in some new piece of equipment, the same Captain would look at it sceptically, put his finger in his mouth, hold it up in the wind, and say, cryptically, "Mejor!"

There are Spanish seamen who would have discovered America without Columbus, and Jose, who has become a friend over the years, is one of those, utterly trustworthy and with a sense of irony black as night and twice as impenetrable. Together with his wife and members of my family we have charted courses which, while they never approach the heroic, are still pretty adventurous for mere amateurs.

Which was the greatest summer? The one in Greece, where each island seemed to have its own excise rules and regulations, and where an underpaid university professor made a small fortune sitting in a cafe translating replies to official questionnaires from one alphabet to another, and sharing the profits with the customs; or the one in Turkey, where the first vision of Istanbul floated like a pink and golden dream several feet above the water-line, laid on a bed of purple mist? Or yet again the one in Yugoslavia, where the rehearsal of a play in a conspiratorial corner of Dubrovnik led me to believe I was watching the *Merchant of Venice,* until the Jewish Merchant declared in an aside that he had accomplished his negotiations with unexpected

"I'm just going to carry the dog around the block."

haste, and that he now had fifteen minutes to spare, and would therefore, as a righteous man, spend it at home waiting for the Messiah! The play turned out to be by the Dalmatian author Dizic, written in 1525, nearly a century before Shakespeare!

I do not know, or care, which was the greatest summer. They were all laid against that wholesome monotony of the sea, that ever-changing sameness which is the finest background of all for the contemplation of eternal verities and the trivialities of the moment. They call the Mediterranean the cradle of civilization, and certainly only a waterway could deserve such a name. Here you plough through the same furrows where Caesar and Hannibal ploughed before you, and stare up at the same sky.

On land, you must subtract the television aerials and the traffic if you wish to imagine how the Colosseum or the Acropolis once stood; at sea, there is no stretch of the imagination needed, for all imagination is stretched. And if you stop a fishing-boat at dawn, and watch your Spanish friend argue in mime with Turkish fishermen about the quality or price of fish, you are back among the Phoenician merchants haggling in the ancient language of signs and enjoying the clash of commercial ingenuities as though it were a game of chance.

I notice that while I was writing those few reflections I have lost my shoes somewhere under my desk. Certainly the salt-mines of Siberia were no place for me, not even as a place to spend a great winter, and to hell with the family fortune.

Oh, What a Not Unsatisfactory War!

The complete military memories of HARRY SECOMBE

Someone said to me recently—on Remembrance Sunday of all days—"Did you have a good war?"

I was appalled, secretly, although I made self-deprecating noises at the time. "How can anyone apart from Mr. Krupps have had a good war?" I thought.

Yet I must confess that I'm the first one to try to teach our four kids how to march in step whenever there's a military band on the box. I've given up trying to teach the wife—she was a tool-setter in the war anyway. There's a joke in there somewhere, I think.

At Regimental Reunions I'm there with the lads, stirring up old memories. "'Ere—d'you remember old Okehampton being caught behind the NAAFI in Aldershot with the ATS Sgt. Major, and saying he didn't mind jankers because he'd just realised his life's ambition?" And remembering that Okehampton's real name was Woodcock.

It is amazing what the mind can be persuaded to forget, especially when reminiscing ex-soldiers get together. Skirmishes become full-scale battles,

retreats turn into strategic withdrawals, molehills become mountains—and when they've finished talking about sex they get on to the War.

I can't honestly say that I loved the War. I was in it but not of it you might say, and yet even at this distance, I remember parts of it with a startling clarity and a certain rueful affection . . .

We were about to embark on the invasion of Sicily and our regiment stood to attention on a sandy parade ground outside Sousse in Tunisia.

Montgomery drove his desert-camouflaged staff car into the middle of our parade. "Bweak wanks and gather wound," he said, waving his fly whisk.

I was pushed along from behind, finishing up right against the car, and directly beneath the great man himself, who now began to address us.

"Take your hats off. I want to see what you look like." I struggled to take off my beret, hot with the knowledge that beneath it lay four months' growth of wiry Welsh hair. It had gone reasonably unnoticed within the fairly lax discipline of a unit actively engaged in battle, but old hawk-eye above me was not going to miss it. To add to the general decrepit nature of my appearance, I was wearing a pair of steel spectacles which had been repaired at the bridge and at both sides with electrician's tape, with the result that the frames sat on my nose at an angle of 45 degrees. To complete my Hammer Horror kit I was also wearing a piece of plaster over a mosquito bite on my chin. My hair, released from its bereted bondage, cascaded over my face and ears in a shower of sand.

Above me Monty was telling us that we of the First Army were now joining the glorious Eighth Army and we had a tradition to keep up. Cautiously I raised my head and looked up at him, trying to look committed to the task ahead.

"We're going to hit the Hun for six," he said, slapping his thigh with his fly whisk. I nodded fervently. The movement seemed to catch his eye and he looked down at me. What he saw seemed to strike him speechless and we stood looking at each other, locked in a moment of time, the two opposite ends of the scale face to face—a glittering Goliath and a dishevelled David, but both on the same side.

I cleared my throat, anxious to break the silence.

"We're with you, sir," I said fatuously. He shook his head slightly, as if awakening from a petit mal, looked away and carried on with his pep talk. But the pep seemed to have gone out of him, and soon, with one last unbelieving glance in my direction he was driven away wearing the expression of a man with something on his mind. He must have been reminded of Wellington's remark when watching a march past of his men—"I don't know what effect these men will have upon the enemy, but, by God, they terrify me."

During my six and a half years in the Army, the only other celebrities I managed to get near to were Spike Milligan, who, like myself at that

"Another damned absentee landlord."

28

"For goodness sake, man! Have you no sense of history?"

time was playing walk-on parts in battles; General Alexander who was playing the lead in the Mediterranean Theatre of War, and Randolph Churchill, whom Sgt. Ferris and myself captured outside Medjaz-el-Bab. He happened to be facing the wrong way at the time, and his paratroop helmet did look Teutonic in the half-light, and besides who could believe a German who claimed to be Winston Churchill's son?

There was the time when our 25-pounder guns clattered into a little town in Southern Italy. We were the first Allied troops the inhabitants had seen and I sat astride my battered Matchless 350 c.c. motor bike like a miniature, mechanised John Wayne. The townsfolk stood either side of the dusty main road waving hastily made Union Jacks and showering us with fruit and flowers from their balconies. The lads in the open trucks were up to their ears in grapes and figs, but I found it difficult to catch anything without letting go of the handlebars. I slowed to a halt, and pretended that I was waving on the traffic.

"Frutta?" I enquired of a buxom signorina leaning from a first floor window. "Si," she said, and knocked me off my bike with a well-aimed pomegranate.

Ah, but life was not all like that. There was one little bit of glory which came my way, though perhaps not the way I expected.

After the fall of Tunis a Victory Parade was held in which our Regiment took part, and having been dismissed as too scruffy for the march-past, I climbed up one of the palm trees lining the route. It was quite near the saluting base, and as there were a couple of cine cameras pointing my way, I tried to wriggle into a position where I could be seen. My movements disturbed a colony of ants living among the leaves and I was too occupied trying to stop them marching up my shorts to pay much attention to the marching below, or to the newsreel cameras.

I wrote home to my parents in my weekly air mail letter that I might be seen on the screen if they looked for a palm tree near the saluting stand. After about three months solid cinema-going my mother finally saw me—well, not all of me, just my left leg. She wrote to say that she was sure it was mine because the stocking was around the ankle and that's how mine always was when I was a boy, and did I get the balaclava helmet and the talcum powder?

I never got around to seeing it myself and I have watched *All Our Yesterdays* on TV in anticipation ever since. I want to point to the screen and say to my kids—"Look, that's my left leg in Tunis." There's not much chance of that now though, they've got up to the post-war period. Pity. I had a good-looking left leg in those days.

29

Last-Tango-in-Paris Do-it-Yourself Kit!

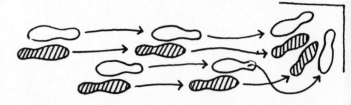
Who wants to see the boring, over-publicised *Last Tango In Paris* when you could have so much more fun making your own version? All you'll need is:—

> 1 lb butter
> 1 empty room
> 1 camera
> 1 old friend, 1 young friend (for doing the acting)
> soap and hot water
> anything else that comes to hand

Explain to your friends that they will be representing two people caught in a sudden frenzy to communicate via their bodies in a moving but doomed relationship, and let them get on with it. (Make sure they realise that the reviews will dwell on the essential innocence and agonised purity of the film: that way you can get away with anything.) Oh, and keep the windows closed. What with gas pressure dropping and everything, the last thing you want is a lead actor with a bad cold and goose pimples.

YOU WILL ALSO NEED 10 HANDY EXCUSES FOR NOT GOING TO SEE "LAST TANGO IN PARIS"

1 "I really can't imagine that any film left uncensored by the French will be worth seeing, do you? After all, we cut three minutes from *Trash*, which was bad enough. The French cut twenty-five minutes. They're probably running it as a short."

2 "There's nobody I know in it."

3 "Strictly between you and me, I hear the music's dreadful."

4 "I saw Marlon Brando's chest in *One-Eyed Jacks*. It wasn't that great."

5 "I haven't read the book but I feel I've seen the movie."

6 "It's only *Lolita* without the dialogue, and that was the only good thing about *Lolita*."

7 "I'm going to wait till Ernie Wise rewrites it as a television play."

8 "A friend of my brother's worked on the film in Paris, and he said that it's not Brando at all on screen, it's an authentic life-size replica of him that they moved slightly between each shot, and I'm not going to pay good money to see the first-ever film with dubbed mumbling."

9 "You don't seriously expect me to go and see yet another film about an American tourist in Paris?"

10 "The children wanted to see it, but I couldn't face it myself."

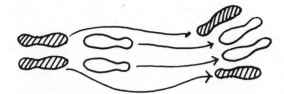

Facing your partner, place your left foot outside her right foot and your right foot outside her left foot. Bend towards her, taking care not to let go. *Keep the knees relaxed.*

Shuffle round the room a bit now, till you are comfortable, placing left foot in front of you, then right foot, then left and so on. Failure to do this may cause falling over. *Do not get out of camera shot.* Now rip her clothes off.

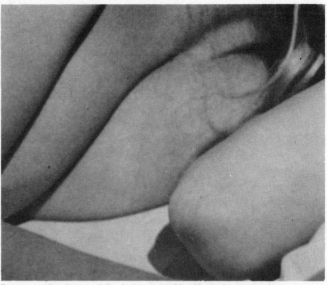

Lots can be done with close-ups of bodies where you're not sure which bit is which. The thing on the right is actually an elbow, or perhaps it's a cucumber.

This is the famous incident where Brando picks up an apple in the thick of the action and surprises everyone by just eating it. What can *you* think of to do with an apple?

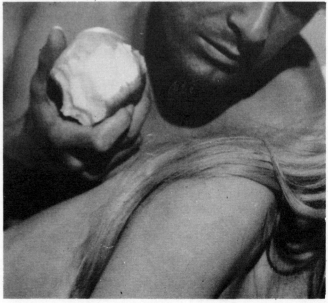

You'll need some sequences like this tender episode where Brando laments his childhood by brutally assaulting the girl.

ALL THE WORLD'S AN AUDIENCE

HEWISON books seats for the tourist invasion of the London theatre

"Of course, the roman à clef is obvious—it depicts the British nation struggling to adjust itself to the realities of its Post-Imperial position. Did you not spot the Queen symbol in the second act? As for the detective—or should I say The Detective?—a little over-emphasised as the All-Seeing God, I thought . . ."

"I said, 'Here comes tomorrow's audience'."

"Inferior British trousers alway falling down. Superior Yohido Garment Inc. will m big killing here."

Back in the Decadent Dump or How to Desert a Cultural Renaissance

by BARRY HUMPHRIES

There's a Cultural Renaissance going on in Australia at the present period of time, and *I'm* not ashamed to be a part of it!" That awe-inspiring statement was flung at me, more in sorrow than in anger, way back in 1965 by some Melbourne Michelangelo when I was about to return to London to resume my sporadic theatrical career. Faced with almost inevitable poverty and failure in a lousy climate I must have seemed perverse, if not mad, just walking out like that on a perfectly good cultural renaissance.

I suppose Sydney Harbour *tastes* not unlike the Gulf of Tuscany and, on a dark night after a surfeit of Chateau Down-Under, the Sydney Harbour Bridge vaguely resembles the Ponte Vecchio. For that matter, Ayres Rock is merely a larger version of Mount Parnassus painted tangerine, and the Sydney Opera House (in 1965 at least) was roofless and rubble-strewn, *just* like the Parthenon!

Similarly my Australian acquaintances were possessed of a Da Vinci-like vigour and versatility. They worked in advertising agencies, wrote telly criticism, reviewed pop records, edited savagely satirical magazines and

Barry Humphries is world famous in Australia and known affectionately to discerning cognoscenti in Britain. Although still incredibly young he has been commuting between Sydney and London for ages, delighting the English-speaking public with his one-man shows, neckties, virtuoso television programmes and deeply learned book reviews. A lover of horses, money and women, his most celebrated creations are Edna Everage (housewife superstar) and, with artist Nick Garland, ex-patriot folk hero Barry Mckenzie, who made his debut in a legendary Private Eye comic strip. A major motion picture "The Adventures of Barry Mckenzie" is currently breaking all box office records in Australia and it will be released in London in June complete with its controversial technicolor scenes of full-frontal chunderings.

"Well, shall we lure him on to the rocks or shan't we?"

sometimes even took photographs. Although they struck terror into the hearts of local philistines and craven expatriates they were so obviously overflowing with creativity one would be foolhardy to reject their invitation and drop out of the downunder renaissance. None the less I did. It was hard to deny energetically that my motives for returning to the Great Wen were to crawl up the backsides of the decadent Poms, rubbish my old mates, and sell Australia short up the length and breadth of Britain.

I had known Australian painters, actors and writers who, having failed to crack it in the Olde Country, had preferred to starve to death in their Holland Park bed-sitters rather than go home and face the scorn and derision of the cultural elite in Melbourne and Sydney. Pining for local lager and lamingtons (an ethnic cake; sponge cubes doused in chocolate icing; and desiccated coconut) they sat before their guttering paraffin heaters quaffing costly Redoxons and staring morosely at their damp-ravaged Qantas posters. To rationalise their ill-fortune they blamed the Brits.

"They're scared silly of us, Bazza," said a wild-eyed duffle-coated Australian film-maker to me once. He was shivering with apoplexy rather than the cold. "As soon as my sister sends me the fare I'm clearing out of this decadent dump. The Poms can't stand our bloody *vitality* and sheer creative bloody *drive!*" he added, sliding languidly from bar stool to Watneyfied Axminster, his fingers barely enclosing the pound I had guiltily lent him.

34

Aussies who have made the big time in England become objects of pity rather than contempt. Rolf Harris, Sidney Nolan, Rupert Murdoch, Scobie Breasley, Joan Sutherland, to name but a few traitors to the Southern Cross have not *really* succeeded, certainly not in an arena where success counts for anything. They've *sold out*! Capitulated to English decadence, the fast sterling quid, and in many instances which shall be nameless, compromised their pure heterosexual Australian bodies. If they really get to be world-famous they cease to be Australians at all. Expatriate is the dirtiest word in the Oz vocabulary. Next to, and often synonymous with, poofdah.

SCENE: The V.I.P. lounge of Sydney airport. Kangaroo fur carpet, sharkskin upholstery, aboriginal motifs on the Japanese vinyl wallpaper, vases of flesh-pink gladdies and trays of piping hot savoury lamingtons and ice-cold sparkling Queensland sherry. An Australian actor returned from moderate success in London faces the Media.

Channel 5: Great to have you back, Bazz! Now you're back in Aussie how much can we expect to see of you?

ACTOR *(suffering from five consecutive champagne breakfasts and acute jet-lag):* I'll only be back for three months, I'm afraid, Ian. Been offered a BBC series.

Channel 5: Yeah. I suppose your old mates seem pretty unsophisticated after the types you're used to rubbing shoulders with over there!

(brief pause for drinks)

Channel 8: Great to have you back, Bazz! Now you're back in the sticks, how much can your old mates expect to see of you? Just a flying visit to syphon off a few dollars then back to Britsville?

ACTOR *(haunted-looking, but quick as a flash):* Cripes no, Colin! I mean, there's a bit of talk about a TV series, but what the hell. It's great to be back. Well, blood's thicker than water, and all this lovely sunshine . . . The beaches . . . Planning to stay on in Sydney indefinitely as a matter of fact. There's a cultural Renaissance going on in Australia at the present period of time, and I'm not ashamed to . . .

Channel 8 *(interrupting with a friendly grin):* That figures, Bazz, that figures. The word's around you're not doing any good over there!

. . .

You can't win in the super-egalitarian society, and it's OK to walk tall in Australia so long as you're no taller than anyone else. And yet, having opted for life in the Decadent Dump, one occasionally experiences a wistful twinge of nostalgia for wholesome renaissance-style living in the Promised Land, flowing with milk-shakes and tomato sauce.

One misses dinner in a smart Adelaide restaurant with the head waiter wearing a dinner jacket over his cardigan and an ice bucket beside the table filled with tinned lager. One misses Brisbane television with its all-night horror movies and all-day horror commercials.

One misses Yugoslav taxi drivers and bank managers in long white socks and bermuda shorts, aerosol snow and plastic holly on stifling Christmas days, and the priority coverage which British royalty still receives in Australian newspapers and magazines. Long after Australians have learned to shuffle patriotically to their feet after the first few inane lyrics of *Waltzing Matilda,* the *Australian Woman's Weekly* will still carry the world's most authoritative documentation of the Windsor family, its dress and doings.

Living in London one also misses a society which is predominantly Anglo-Saxon; one pines for all those faces, sun-bronzed albeit white. Of course, the pressure of dwelling in the surging centre of a fully fledged cultural renaissance has taken its toll of the once healthy and robust Antipodean. Next to his Australian cousin the Englishman seems trimmer and more rested. A meatless diet, and the admirable London custom of commencing the

"I only just made it before my Dad's vasectomy."

35

weekend on Friday and starting the business week on Tuesday makes for a more relaxed and ulcer-free white-collar population. The sensible habit of working in the office from 10.30 a.m. till noon and then from 3.15 p.m. till 4.30 p.m. with a civilized break for lunch, of leaving the phone off the hook or never bothering to answer it, all these deeply-ingrained customs keep the British businessman clear of eye, fresh-complexioned and free of those neuroses which afflict the frenetic work-crazed Aussies.

Poms who migrate to Australia usually survive if they remember to swim between the flags, but if the sharks don't get them, the pace and the protein will. Ten swift frosties and a stand-up under-done tournedos isn't the Englishman's idea of a healthy lunch-break, and he's usually just started to pick at his prawn and pineapple omelette when the lamington trolley swings into view.

Australians are either eating in a hurry, or transporting tucker to their luxury bungalows in the suburbs. A nice little Brit migrant I know got a job driving a Melbourne taxi. One evening last month he picked up the Archetypal Australian-in-a-hurry outside a pub laden with parcels. Falling into the back seat of the enormous Holden the fare said:

"Take us home for cripes sake, sport! Have you got room in the cab for twenty beers and three dozen oysters?"

"Bung 'em on the front seat if you like mate," said the obliging Brit.

His intoxicated passenger put his chin over the edge of the upholstery and copiously did so. It took two cops and a bucket of Dettol to clear the cab.

I suppose one man's taxi is another man's vomitorium, and even a Renaissance society has odd moments of something like decadence. For those of us who can't make up our minds whether we prefer the English or the Australian variety there's always Marrakesh or Manila with extra lengthy siestas and faulty telephones to suit the Poms, and for the delectation of displaced Aussies, plenty of taxis with convenient Jumbo-sized bucket seats.

"It took some time but finally we got him house-trained."

JONATHAN ROUTH: *Calling all*
A.A. members—this is your interpreter speaking

AA Members Handbook 1972/73.
Automobile Association. 60p.

I quote from this work, the Yellow Book of our day:

> ★★★★★ **Claridges** Brook St W1 ☎01-629 8860
> 205rm(205⇌) Lift D 📺 TV ✠ Ldmidnight
> B⇌£15.10 L£2.85alc D£3alc S15%

So, let us now be very patient and interpret.

It's a five-star place (more appropriate really if five crowns had been used), it has a name, an address, and a telephone number.

> ★★★★★ **Claridges** Brook St W1 ☎01-629 8860
> 205rm(205⇌) Lift D 📺 TV ✠ Ldmidnight
> B⇌£15.10 L£2.85alc D£3alc S15%

It has 205 bedrooms, and 205 men permanently soaking in baths. Unless this is a pictorial euphemism for 205 lavatory attendants. Or maybe it means there's a framed reproduction of that picture of the Murder of Marat in his Bath on the wall of each of the 205 bedrooms. Or that when all the 205 bedrooms are full the staff will be happy to make up beds in baths for a further 205 guests. The meaning of this symbol is not crystal clear. It's the first time that the AA have branched out into this form of artwork, and I suspect they gave their artist too free a hand. Why is the man in the bath? Surely the sort of person who goes to Claridges is not accustomed to storing coal in his bath and therefore needs this clue as to the correct use of the receptacle? I find it baffling. The man himself looks surprised, as though he's been caught doing in the bath something people don't normally do in the bath. The AA Disciplinary Committee would do well to consider his continued appearance in their handbook.

We continue:

> ★★★★★ **Claridges** Brook St W1 ☎01-629 8860
> 205rm(205⇌) Lift D 📺 TV ✠ Ldmidnight
> B⇌£15.10 L£2.85alc D£3alc S15%

Claridges has a lift. Good. But it's a lift followed by a moon symbol—a romantic lift, for lovers; it operates only at night; Juliet's balcony gliding up and down the Brook Street facade of the hotel.

Or, the liftman's a loony. "The lift has stopped, sir, not as you suggest through my turning off the current, but because of a genuine mechanical failure. And it's laid down in regulations, sir, that the procedure to be adopted in such a circumstance is for the lift operator and all passengers to strip off all their clothes and do heavy breathing until rescued. See, sir, with my previous experience I can completely undress in 23 seconds flat . . ."

But it isn't that. The moon symbol means there's a Night Porter on duty. With any luck he's a loony, too. You'll know for sure if he turns out to be the man lying in your bath.

> ★★★★★ **Claridges** Brook St W1 ☎01-629 8860
> 205rm(205⇌) Lift D 📺 TV ✠ Ldmidnight
> B⇌£15.10 L£2.85alc D£3alc S15%

On.

This is more difficult. A section of accordion I would guess. It means the loony night porter can be summoned to come to your room and play the instrument—if he's not occupied in serenading couples travelling in the lift by moonlight, that is . . . Or does it simply mean central heating, a radiator? If you still want an accordion that's the first place I'd look behind.

> ★★★★★ **Claridges** Brook St W1 ☎01-629 8860
> 205rm(205⇌) Lift D 📺 TV ✠ Ldmidnight
> B⇌£15.10 L£2.85alc D£3alc S15%

TV—that's simple enough. An old-fashioned entertainment for those who don't want to get involved with the loony accordionist. But wait. It's followed by an impaled dog's head. Definitely a dog of the hound variety. They are eccentric, some of the old county families who put up at Claridges. "I've told you, Sir Jocelyn, you may stable your horse in the mews behind, but we cannot allow the public corridors of the second floor or the television lounge to be used as an exercise pen for a whole pack of hounds . . ."

I suspect the AA is trying to suggest that Claridges reserves the right to adopt stern measures against patrons who try to smuggle in packs of hounds.

> ★★★★★ **Claridges** Brook St W1 ☎01-629 8860
> 205rm(205⇌) Lift D 📺 TV ✠ Ldmidnight
> B⇌£15.10 L£2.85alc D£3alc S15%

So we come to Ldmidnight—Ladies are expected to be out of Gentlemen's Rooms by Midnight, surely? It's good to discover there are still places in the permissive society where the old standards are adhered to. They can't be serious, can they? No. "Ldmidnight" (pronounced "DIEKNEE") is a delicious Norwegian cheese, the speciality of Room Service ever since the late King Olaf demanded 14 kilos of it for breakfast. It's the traditional food of travelling Norwegian accordionists, and you will find tidbits of Ldmidnight brought on when the loony night porter comes to play in your room.

Sadly, if we refer to Abbreviations and Symbols we find that the prefix "Ld" means the time last dinner can be ordered. But you can still ask if they've got some Norwegian cheese.

And just before the prices, which make as much sense as any prices do these days, we get this big B followed by that man in the bath again. Obviously—breakfast served in your bath.

I said the fellow looked as though he was doing something one doesn't normally do in the bath. Digesting his kipper off a plate on his knee. The place is bulging with eccentrics.

Claridges, from this account, just isn't how I imagined it at all. These roaming packs of hounds, crazy accordionists, loony liftmen. It's surprising how much extraordinary information they can pack into these brief entries in the Handbook.

"I don't want to get well."

Case No. 456/37/A, Filed under Office Politics *being one of the light*

clerical duties of KEITH WATERHOUSE

As Personnel Records will confirm, I have been in the employ of this Company man and boy for twenty-five years, so I feel I owe a word of explanation as to why I am about to do myself in during the firm's time. Also, why I am writing this suicide note—copies to Mng Director, Sales Supervisor, Coroner, Wife, Accounts Dept and Personnel Records—on the firm's letterhead. This latter act, as I hope to make clear, is symbolic.

We must go back to the Brown Envelopes Scandal of 1963 to understand the workings of my deranged mind. Mr. Jefferson's memo to all depts, dated 4/9/63, refers. In that memo—or ultimatum, as some of us preferred to call it—Mr. Jefferson, then newly jumped-up as Stationery Supervisor, laid down that in the interests of standardisation the three sizes of white manilla envelope then in use were to be called in, and 9in by 4in brown envelopes henceforth employed for all purposes.

There were various reactions to this edict. A majority of what we might call "company men" simply toed the party line and returned their white envelopes to stores forthwith. The bolshie element seized the opportunity to carry off white envelopes wholesale in briefcase or sandwich-box. The drifters among us merely ignored the order, using brown or white envelopes as the fit took them.

There was, however, a strong splinter group, centred mainly here in the after-sales dept, which queried the whole thinking behind Jefferson's decision. What, we asked, would happen to the white envelopes after they had been called in? Would they be sold as waste paper or would they, as some of us suspected, be left to rot in a basement storage cupboard like the wartime economy labels which are now all stuck together and unfit for use?

It was clear to me that Jefferson had not followed his policy through. I did not object to brown envelopes in any way, form or shape whatsoever; that I wish to put on record. But if we were to move into a brown envelope era, surely the transition could have been effected gradually *as and when the white envelopes were used up.*

I admit that insofar as I had any authority in after-sales—I was at that time No. 2 to Ponsonby—I encouraged the staff here to continue using white envelopes until supplies ran down. In so doing I fell foul of Ponsonby's then secretary, Miss Hopkinshaw, who was strictly in favour of playing the Jefferson memo by the book. Miss Hopkinshaw and I had already crossed swords over an electric kettle in the filing cabinet; it was not a happy time for me.

We now come to the events of 1970, and it is necessary to sketch in the background of that fateful year. Ponsonby has had his heart attack and I

"Permission to go ashore, sir?"

have stepped into his shoes; Davenport has retired, leaving a vacancy as sales director which is filled by Moody; Jefferson, to the general astonishment, takes Moody's place in Admin. Otterby takes over from Jefferson. Meanwhile Miss Hopkinshaw has also been ascending the ladder—we will not ask how. No longer a secretary but now a personal assistant, she throws in her lot with Jefferson. Thus it was that the Jefferson-Hopkinshaw axis was already lined up against me when the Hatstand Crisis of June 1970 split the office in two.

The Hatstand Crisis had its roots in the historic decision to turn the sales floor into one great office on the open-plan system. That particular bone of contention has already been well-gnawed; suffice it to say that when walls had been pulled down and partitions carted away, the office was seen to be dotted with hatstands. What had previously been private perquisites were now public impedimenta; the hatstands had been pitched into the arena of controversy.

The after-sales staff were evenly divided: between those who did not wear hats and those who did wear hats; between those who slung their raincoats over a chair and those who had been brought up to look after their clothes properly; between those who tripped over the hatstands and those who had the elementary sense to look where they were going.

For my part, I was in favour of compromise. I argued powerfully in favour of stacking the hatstands in groups of six at various strategic points around the office, where their sheer bulk would discourage further accidents. Failing

*"Dick, I'm **sure** it's a burglar!
Run down and demand his resignation!"*

that, why not range the hatstands along the wall, out of harm's way? Let reason prevail.

At the end of the day, I was unable to sway my colleagues. I recall a colourful phrase of my No. 2, Gomersall, on the day he sprained his ankle. I will not repeat it here, but it was to the effect that the hatstands should be disposed of. Very well: I would compromise further. Let the hatstands be removed *on condition that the management provide us with hooks and coathangers.*

I should stress that this was strictly an internal issue, and one which I had every confidence we in after-sales could solve among ourselves, given time. What I did not bargain for was that Gomersall was a near-neighbour of Jefferson's. That Gomersall inspired the Jefferson memo of 11/6/70 I have no doubt at all; they were seen in the public house together the evening before. Jefferson had but recently taken over in Admin, and he would have seized eagerly on the hatstand issue as a means of making his presence felt, as well as persecuting me personally.

The 11/6/70 memo spelled the kiss of death for hatstands. They were, pronounced Jefferson, an anomaly in an open-plan office. They had to go.

If he thought I proposed to lock horns with him on such a peripheral issue, he was mistaken. I "played it cool". As my memo of 17/6/70 (copy attached) makes clear, I agreed to Jefferson's proposals on the understanding that the management would provide the hooks and coat-hangers already mooted in my informal discussions with the after-sales staff.

Jefferson countered this ploy with the notorious memo of 18/6/70—composed, as I happen to know, by his side-kick Miss Hopkinshaw. "My only concern is to remove the hatstands, which have become a hazard," he wrote. "As far as this department is concerned, you may have all the hooks and coat-hangers your heart desires, but it just so happens these are a matter for Maintenance, which is i/c office stores, and not for Admin."

I had him in the palm of my hand. For if hooks and coat-hangers were the responsibility of Maintenance, it followed as surely as night follows day that *so were hatstands.* Jefferson had no authority whatever to remove those hatstands. Nevertheless, in a spectacular early-morning coup the next day, that is precisely what he did. My memo dated 19/6/70, copy to Mng Director, refers.

It is not for me to speculate on the relationship between Miss Hopkinshaw and the Managing Director. All I can say is that before the week was out it was made known that Maintenance, hitherto responsible for hooks, coat-hangers and hatstands, was to be brought under the umbrella of Admin. So were Staff Catering, Welfare and—more significantly—Stationery Supplies. Jefferson's empire-building had begun in earnest.

Of the Carbon Paper Affair of 1972 I will say nothing. The change from blue to black carbon paper was ostensibly Otterby's initiative, but I think I recognise the hand behind it. When Otterby had his nervous breakdown this month, Jefferson and his lackey Miss Hopkinshaw came into the open. A memo (pp Jefferson, but signed in his absence by Miss so-called Hopkinshaw) instructed all departmental heads that a multi-use internal envelope was henceforth to be used for internal memoranda. The practice of using office envelopes, that is to say the brown 9in by 4in issue as authorised on 4/9/63, was to cease. And so we had come full circle.

But there was more. The unauthorised practice of using office letterheads for internal correspondence, instead of the standard memorandum form that may be obtained by application in the first instance to Mr. Bighead Jefferson, was also discouraged. Furthermore—I am referring now to a private memo from Jefferson, though not, I may say, written on any standard memorandum form, far from it—any further rumours which I may spread about him and

40

Miss Hopkinshaw and their activities in the night safe, although admittedly not in office hours, would lead to serious repercussions.

I was in a cleft stick, and still am. Beaten by the system, I am too old to seek another post. I certainly cannot carry on as Head of after-sales. I therefore tender my resignation on this, the office letterhead of the company. The Welfare Dept, under the aegis of Mr. Jefferson, will find me hanging from the Advance Towel Supply unit in the No. 4 cloakroom. It is my last wish that the Managing Director may be present, so that he may observe at first hand the state of that cloakroom since Jefferson took over.

*"Just **had** to drop back to tell you again what a **great** party it was—**great** party."*

Would <u>You</u> Marry Enoch's Daughter

The only thing wrong with having the exclusively coloured suburbs forecast by Enoch Powe
is that they might turn out to be just like the all-white suburbs, says MAHOOD

"I'm afraid it looks as if Moslems, Hindus and Buddhists aren't very good church goers either!"

*"Thank you Robert Dougall for giving the white version of the news, now for **our** version."*

*"The fact that someone is Jewish is immaterial and the fact that he is white is immaterial but we can't have a member who is both Jewish **and** white!"*

"If I had known we were going to be the Token Whites
I wouldn't have come!"

". . . and in this policy you are given
full comprehensive cover against
your house losing value through
whites moving in next door!"

"For heaven's sake, Carmen, you
know what the sight of a coloured
woman can do to these whites!"

"I think we should take them for a quick drive through Hampstead
soon—after all, they've got to see whites **sometime**!"

How to be a Man in '73

by ANN LESLIE

"Dumb broads with big knockers—that's what guys go for. Always have. Always will," my friend Irwin informed me recently as he crouched over his diet-soda in the Beverly Hills Hotel, stabbing glumly at the cocktail olives with a diamond stick-pin. "But what the hell do *women* go for these days? I'm telling you, in all sincerity, Ann, I just do not know any more."

And Irwin needs to know, because Irwin is a Hollywood talent scout whose job it is to feed male and female sex-symbol fodder into the grinding molars of his studio's production machine. Thanks to male conservatism on such matters, selecting suitable broads has always been a doddle: Irwin simply keeps on herding Pasadena Carnival Queens and Kansas Kup-Kake Kuties into the studio compound, where their teeth are fixed and their knockers siliconised and they're taught how to pronounce "Shop-en-hower" so they'll know what to say when reporters quiz them on their favourite bedside reading.

Picking guys used to be a doddle too. In Irwin's early days, what it took to be a man as far as women were concerned, was a chiselled chin, short-back-and-sides and a noble soul. Thus Irwin's discoveries spent much of their celluloid time heading into studio blizzards in fits of terminal self-sacrifice or going down in battleships saying, "When all this is over, Kowalski, promise me one thing: promise me you'll go see Lydia and tell her from me, 'There'll always be peach-blossom for us.' She'll understand . . ." And she did, and we did, and a good weep was had by all.

After a while, of course, this *chevalier sans reproche* began to pall and Hollywood reckoned we broads were now ready for a spot of meatier fare. Enter the era of "Einstein He Ain't", as in "Einstein he ain't, but he's gotta whole lotta balls"—Irwin's description of one of his protégés, which the blushing hulk concerned rightly took to be a compliment.

The new ideal was, like Esau, a hairy man, and hordes of likely lads were scooped out of Mid-West gas-stations and Appalachian lumber-camps and deposited in piles outside Central Casting. The studio gave them names like Thug Masterson, taught them how to mumble, "A man's gotta do what a man's gotta do," and issued them with directives on the etiquette of not eating peas off their knives or cleaning out their ears in public with rolled up fan-letters.

The heart-throb market was now cornered by Cro-Magnon throwbacks with brains like butter-beans and hands like boiled hams. Actually, sex-symbol-wise I've always found this specimen to be highly resistible, especially when he later progressed to wearing Savile Row suits and shoulder-holsters and started giving tedious orders about his vodka-martinis. Tossing ladies into piranha ponds like bits of old cheese-sandwich may seem

the last word in witty sexual behaviour to men, but to this woman at any rate, it's a definite erotic no-no.

Be that as it may, amorous youth from Bude to Panama gazed up at this muscle-bound stud, hung about with ecstatic blondes, and came to the conclusion that the surest way to a maiden's heart was via the chest-expander.

But alas, no sooner had biceps begun to swell like puffer-fish beneath the world's sweat-shirts then the image-makers sniffed the wind of change, found it smelled of grass, and, in *Variety's* phrase, briefly went boffo for the sesame-seed set.

Out went Superstud, in came spotty poets with concave chests, and adenoidal minstrels given to singing limp little threnodies on the evil of strip-mining. The day of the seven-stone weakling had dawned at last and Sunset Boulevard was suddenly full of redundant Thugs, Tabs, Rips and Rocks trying to disguise themselves as the Now Generation behind Indian head-bands and copies of the *Whole Earth Catalogue*.

They needn't have bothered for lo, the songs of the flower-people have faded away, the brown rice is shrivelled and gone, and the voice of the liberated woman is now heard in our land.

And judging by her theme-song, the way to this lady's heart is to recognise that a man's place is now in the home shovelling strained-beef dinners into squalling infants, while she's off asset-stripping

45

"Dear Sir, this is the first letter I have ever felt compelled to write to a newspaper . . ."

or rapping with her revolutionary sisters. "Role-reversal" is the name of the game, and think what fun it'll be spending your life seeing the wife off on the 8.15 to Waterloo before settling down to your cosy beer mornings with nice Mr. Crowley from next door.

Of course, as with any role, you must remember the stage directions and not ad-lib too much. For example, when the middle-aged managing directress whisks you off in her Rolls to a candle-lit dinner, don't let on you're taking a degree in tropical agronomy—or if you do, try to keep cool when she murmurs "My, my, whatever is a lovely young fellow like you bothering his handsome head with big words like that for?" When she

"He's been deposed."

interrupts your brilliant analysis of the world currency crisis with "Has anyone ever told you before what beautiful eyes you've got," resist the urge to shove her face in the soup, snarling "Of course they have, you stupid old bag!"

And above all when she gets maudlin over the brandy, starts eyeing your crotch, and saying her husband doesn't understand her, try to refrain from blowing smoke in her eyes and snapping coldly, "So what's new, sister?"

Observing these simple rules of the game will ensure that you get a lot of free nosh, though be warned that any woman who's lashed out on a rubbery steak and a bottle of Famagusta Spumante will tend to assume she's thereby purchased your services for the night. So when she drives you home and asks to come in for a "cup of coffee" prepare to leap smartly out of the car, keeping your zip out of grabbing distance and say sweetly "Whatever-made-you-think-I-was-that-kind-of-boy Mrs. Rosenbloom?" Of course, if Mrs. R. happens to be your boss you'll probably find your chances of promotion will plummet for good, but that's just one of the penalties of being a sex-object who doesn't come across with the goods when required . . .

Well, okay, so the sexual revolution hasn't quite come to this pass yet. Perhaps it never will; perhaps liberated woman speak with forked tongue, since apparently it's *not* the dutiful little husband in the pinny with cake-crumbs in his hair who turns the lady on, but nice old-fashioned hunks of male chauvinist pig. A startlingly documented New York survey recently reported that today's top career-woman likes nothing better than to relax after a hard day in the office with something big and stupid picked up off a building site. One lady editor confessed to getting her kicks by bedding down the cabbies who brought her home from her trendy intellectual parties; militant feminists of "good upbringing" were quoted as saying they spent their evenings hanging about working-men's bars sizing up the talent; a woman writer waxed lyrical on the delights of seducing truck-drivers.

And while white-collar woman is off getting her goodies by kerb-crawling and yanking hod-carriers off the scaffolding, what's white-collar man up to? Well, he's apparently round at his analyst's, twitching away about his Identity Problem. According to psychiatrist Dr. George Ginsberg, Women's Lib has caused a massive sexual crisis in America and what he calls "the new impotence" has replaced hernias and heart disease as the middle-class male's most fashionable disease.

So this broken reed will not be encouraged to

hear that *Cosmopolitan* has just decided that "the cult of the violent lover could very well become the sexual phenomenon of the seventies". To prove the point they called on such witnesses as "groover Terence Stamp" who says, "There's nothing like a tasty right-hander to bring them into line," and the inescapable Michael Caine who affirms, "slapping a woman is okay but never be heavy-handed about it. It is a delicate art. The fine brush-work of a beautiful love affair." (Anyone trying that kind of fine brushwork on *me* can look forward to collecting a disability pension for a start.)

The trouble is, with advice like this, is that it's not easy to tell, until you've tried it out, exactly which woman likes being thumped like a dinner-gong and which is liable to scream the street down.

Besides, you may feel that pulling the "Me Tarzan. You Jane" bit will merely inspire shrieks of raucous mirth from the Jane concerned when she knows for a fact that you work in the Pensions department of the White Fish Authority and live with your mother in Penge.

So what do you do? You could, of course, forget the whole silly business and sublimate your energies by growing giant hollyhocks or playing power-politics in the Ferret-Fancy.

Or, of course, you could console yourself with the fact that one woman's meat was ever another woman's poison and that somewhere, some woman is bound to turn up and vote you her personal Flavour of the Month. So keep on truckin', boys, and worry not: as my lapel button puts it, "Trust in God, She Will Provide".

47

"*Man, I really got the Blues,
there's a waiting list for that new Rolls.*"

*HEATH tells it
the way it is*

"*The world is alive with the sound of music . . .*"

"It takes a group like that to make me rethink my position in a capitalistic society."

"When will they stop
The war
The faceless ones
Wait a minute
They have . . .
We'll have to
Sing
About something
Else."

"Man that's a real freaky group."

"I'm white
I wish I was black
That's why I'm blue."

MEATH

"WE HAVE SEEN "THE LIONS OF LONGLEAT

. . . and, cry
ALAN COREN
and DICKINSON,
lived to tell the tale

He was standing outside the hut when I arrived, looking up at the dawn sky, and sniffing adroitly. The wind blew fresh across the little clearing, carrying with it the unmistakable gamey smell of the Victoria and Albert Museum, a hundred yards or so upwind and just discernible through the dense lamp-posts.

We shook hands, a little self-consciously; he, like most of his kind, as if touching a white man for the first time.

"Good morning," he said.

"Good morning, Ngdickinson," I said, "I trust your in-laws thrive."

"I trust your in-laws thrive, bwana," said Ngdickinson. He seemed faintly ill-at-ease in the Western clothes these chaps affect, the old raincoat knotted ineptly about the wiry little frame, the feet oddly large in their unfamiliar shoes. "You are a little late, bwana."

"I have come from Hampstead," I replied, indicating the direction with a sweep of my arm. I knew he could have no conception of it, but it was a courtesy and, as such, important. "The way was hard. The drivers do not like to come this far south."

He lit an evil-looking cigarette and nodded.

"It is here we get the transport," he said. "I have hired a Volkswagen."

"Any special reason?" I asked.

He looked away. His mind seemed to be elsewhere. He might have shrugged.

"It will be better," was all he would say.

We went out to the car, Ngdickinson carrying the gear, my trusty Reporter's Special notebook, with the coil-back and the quick-action leaf-flick, and the two trusty felt pens, made for me by a little man in Japan, one black, one, for when the going gets tricky, red. He also carried his own bag with the traditional kit these fellows have always used, simple but effective sharpened sticks, four heavy 2B's, four light but razor-pointed HB's, and the big green eraser on a string around his neck to ward off error. He also carried his own food, a little oblong piece of compressed nourishment which local people believe will help them work, rest, and play.

He looked at the sky again.

"We must hurry, bwana," he murmured, "before the rains come."

I started the plucky little engine, and pulled out of the clearing in front of the Avis hut, and into the quaintly named Cromwell Road, a relic of colonial splendour which is no more than an ill-made track packed with local traffic and crowded with jabbering native drivers screaming furiously at one another.

But within the hour we were in open country, and the level plains of Slough stretched away on either side. It was then that the winds began. At the first terrible buffet, Ngdickinson was hurled against me.

"March winds and April showers," chanted Ngdickinson.

"March winds and April showers," I replied.

And then the rains hit us.

"They are early this year," said Ngdickinson.

"Perhaps the gods are angry," I suggested.

"I blame Concorde," said Ngdickinson. "It is stirring it all up, bwana. The people do not like it."

"With respect, Ngdickinson," I said, "they are a simple folk. They do not understand."

Ngdickinson looked away, through the pelting waters.

"It goes bang in the sky," he said, quietly.

I consulted the map that he was holding upside down.

"We shall leave the main track at Sutton Benger," I said, "and cut due south across country."

His stubby fingers traced out the native villages of our route, slowly and haltingly.

"Sut-ton Ben-ger," he said, "Yat-tol Key-nell, Urch-font, Pease-down Saint John, Limp-ley Stoke." He shook his head. "These are strange names, bwana. I do not like these names. They are not the names of my people."

"Who are your people, Ngdickinson?"

He sighed.

"I am from Southport, bwana. The women have big bums and speak liltingly. It is far from here, and there are no lions. We drink much thick beer."

I knew he was trying to tell me something. We stopped at Melksham, at a little native inn, and went inside. The wind was mad. We drank two pints of an unfamiliar liquid, and ate some little flakes of potato, but they tasted of bacon and cheese, and Ngdickinson grew nervous, fearing spells. So we drove on again, through the pelting monsoon and under the low black sky; and near to the place called Warminster, I heard a strange sound.

"The big end is going, Ngdickinson," I said, "this could be very serious, in strange country."

"That is my stomach, bwana," said Ngdickinson. "My people eat much at dinner time, which is what we call it when the sun stands straight up."

So we stopped and fed, and the native people stared at us as Ngdickinson ate after the manner of his tribe, who set great store by the elbow. And afterwards, I helped him across to the car and strapped him in, and as he sang softly we lurched out of Warminster and down the last four miles to Longleat, which is where the wild country begins.

There are great gates across the track, and a little hut where a man takes money, and in return gives you a label to stick on the car so that men may know you have passed this way and seen the lions. We left him there, wondering whether we should ever see him again.

Up the hill, under an oak tree, there were eight giraffe and six zebra, sheltering from the rain like bizarre golfers. We stopped, and got out, and one of the Longleat White Hunters, as they are called, came up to us.

"Funny things, giraffes," he said. "Don't loik going in the sheds when it rains. They loik watchin' things. That big 'un up there's named Virginia, arter Lady Bath."

"Been a White Hunter long?" I asked.

"Coupla years," he said, his accent heavily Wilts. "Useter look arter cows. Not much difference, really. You can talk to giraffes an' all. Got to shout a bit louder, what with the ears bein' right up there. Zebbers is soddin' dim, though."

I pointed towards two huge items, like hirsute trucks.

"Nina and Frederik," said the White Hunter. "Ankole cattle, them are. Ain't moved in four months." The wind gusted, shrieking, and the White Hunter shook his head. "It's the giraffes feels the cold most. Stands to reason. They don't start gettin' no flesh on the bone till you're eight feet up."

"Ah," I said. I narrowed my eyes to slits with which to rake the far horizon, upon which, I discovered, a man was whitewashing an outhouse. "We're after lion, actually."

"Through the monkey jungle," said the White Hunter.

We got back in.

"Hallo," I said.

"I am afraid I have trodden in something, bwana," said Ngdickinson. "I believe it is giraffe."

"We may have to use Hertz in future, Ngdickinson," I said, and let in the clutch.

The monkeys, in their own compound, paid little attention to us at first, preferring to sit huddled in small groups of four, which, given the soft, Wiltshire undulations that obtain in that part of the jungle, strongly suggested a whist drive to be followed, no doubt, by cucumber sandwiches and a short disquisition by the hostess on the problem of unsightly facial hair. I stopped the car, and Ngdickinson stealthily selected an HB from his armoury. It was at that moment that a head depended, upside down, from the top of the windscreen. In the first split second—hunters will know how the mind plays strange tricks at such times—I found myself wondering how Ngdickinson had got on to the roof without opening the door. It was then that the animal climbed down and began jumping up and down on the bonnet, jabbering shrilly. Its little hands plucked at the windscreen wipers, whanging them back against the glass.

"It has an enormous whatsit, bwana," cried Ngdickinson, opening up excitedly with his HB, "perhaps, if you will hand me the Polaroid camera, we might capture, I mean, people may accuse this humble artist of exagger—"

"It appears to be sucking the chromework!" I exclaimed, and indeed the animal had applied its mouth to the windscreen washers. It stopped, and banged on the window, and sucked again, and looked at us again.

"Press the button, bwana," said Ngdickinson.

The monkey trapped the jet of water, drank, and then began ambling about looking for trophies. It tugged at the headlamps, it rattled the number plate,

"It's unwise to leave the car when his Lordship is collecting the takings, sir."

"Of course, sir, if you'd like to step round to the back . . ."

it sought, shrieking, to remove the VW emblem. It was then that we noticed the other monkeys watching it, and that they all carried some piece of equipment dislodged from earlier expeditions: radio aerials were much in evidence, several of the smaller citizens were carrying brakelights, and one elderly baboon, who no doubt wore the thing as a seal of office, had a fanbelt round his neck. They were clearly subjecting our monkey to some sort of initiation rite; when he climbed down again, empty-handed they all looked away from him, and he sat apart, ostentatiously mining a nit, but no doubt riven with chagrin.

"It is much like the world, bwana," reflected Ngdickinson, and I looked at him with new respect.

As we came out of the monkey jungle, a bulldozer was gently shoving a rhino up a shallow slope, against a background of blowing elms. It might have been a scene by Constable, had it not been totally different from anything he ever did.

There were elephant there, too, one of which was carrying a newspaper.

We drove down the hill, trusting that Spring did not bring out the worst in pachyderms. Rhino have notoriously rotten eyesight, and the possibility of our Volkswagen's suddenly catching the fancy of a bull in rut was never far from our thoughts. Apart from anything else, I had not examined the small print in the insurance policy too closely, but was prepared to bet that the relevant clause was unlikely to figure in it.

At the bottom of the hill, and through two gates, lay the object of our search. YOU ARE NOW IN LION COUNTRY cried the sign, IF IN TROUBLE, SOUND YOUR HORN AND WAIT FOR THE WHITE HUNTER.

We drove in.

The lions lay draped in the lower branches of ash and oak, or ambled about like tired junkies, blinking and uncaring, or stood licking one another in an absent-minded way. And, as the interior of the car had grown warm with the low-gear grinding and the constant injunctions to keep the windows shut, I opened my quarter-light a fraction.

It was as if a streak of lightning had shot through the compound at shoulder height. Immediately, the heavy leonine lids snapped open, the great shaggy heads reared up from the forepaws, the huge khaki muzzles began to twitch and traverse like radar scanners. And having sought, and sniffed the wind, they began to home in. First they simply glared at us. Then they rose.

"Oh God!" cried Ngdickinson. "It is the giraffe they are smelling, bwana!"

I engaged first gear.

"Throw them the shoe, Ngdickinson!" I shouted.

"It is a new Hush Puppy!" cried Ngdickinson. "Sound the horn!"

But when I pressed that place where, in my own car, there is a horn button, the lights of the Volkswagen came on, silently.

We were doing close to fifty when we got to the gate, down a track like Brighton beach. A White Hunter came out, in a thick cardigan and a bush hat on back to front.

"There's a fifteen moil-an-hour limit," he said.

"Tell that to the lions," I said.

He looked up the road. About a dozen lions were watching us from the top of the hill.

"'Ere," he said, "you ain't bin interferin' with they, 'as you?"

"No," I said.

He furrowed his Wiltshire brow.

"Just loik pigs, they are," he said. "Things upsets 'em."

It snowed on the trek home, icy slush lathering the windscreen which African monkeys had so recently licked. I thought of the lions back there, staring into the English sleet and dreaming of giraffe.

54

And how do I sell THIS to the Common Market?

Easy. You simply remember that, for sales convenience, Europe is now divided into six marketing zones of ascending size and importance. Start at the bottom and work up, as you acquire confidence and off-load your product. Go first to the smallest which is known as

LUXEMBOURG

Do not, whatever else you do, suggest that Luxembourg is small. Most reps try to fit Luxembourg in between a Belgian breakfast and Dutch tea. Fatal. Turn up for your appointment twenty-four hours late, dishevelled, explaining that you have been wandering round the Duchy, lost, trying to find the place. Drop into your conversation phrases like "as tiny as Liechtenstein" or "of course, I've never been to France myself."

When asked for details about the product, stress that you intend to make Luxembourg the springboard for your continental operations. If, translation being what it is, they deduce that you make springboards, encourage them. Sooner or later they will reveal what they really want, at which point you reveal that that's what you make, in aerosol packs. Hint ever so gently that your spray-on product makes things that little bit bigger.

Send them a postcard saying that you have been disappointed by the smallness of

BELGIUM

In Brussels, you will be surprised to find that they have been told along the grapevine that you make spray-on springboards. Smile, shrug and say "Ah, ces Luxembourgeois!"

Market research among the Belgian consumers at their favoured purchasing point (Folkestone) reveals that they will buy anything as long as it is cheaper than at home. Does this invalidate your mission? Not at all. Simply add stickers saying DIRECTEMENT DE FOLKESTONE and charge what you like.

When asked for details about your product, profess absolute secrecy in case the specifications should leak to their great rival.

HOLLAND

The Dutch, as the consumers of Holland are known, speak perfect English and resent it if you try to speak Dutch, which suggests they are not part of the international scene.

As the Dutch are unusually conscious of cleanliness, health and safety standards, stress that your product is non-toxic, lead-free, non-staining, colourless, safe for children and absolutely non-injurious to tulips. Demonstrate this by producing an aerosol, spraying it into the air and saying, "You see?"

When, despite respect for Britain, you are asked for details concerning your product, launch into broad Cockney. Say: "Well, blimey, that's a right teaser and no fooling, search me, governor, you've got me over a barrel; pull the other one, it's got bells on". No self-respecting Dutchman will admit he doesn't know what you've said, so chalk up your order and move on to the most challenging area so far,

ITALY

Psychological analysis of the Italian consumer reveals that he divides his time between loving his mother, fearing his wife and pinching English girls, which casts no light at all on the potential of aerosol packs in the Italian market, though it certainly suggests new theories concerning the mysterious smile on the face of the Mona Lisa. In fact, rather than discuss your banal product, why not launch into a sophisticated discussion of Leonardo da Vinci? Not only will this distract Italian buyers from the details of your product, it will also draw attention to the most famous Italian of all time who was in addition undeniably queer, which will by implication call into question your buyer's virility. If he should wish to change the subject, switch to Michelangelo, that enthusiast of young boys. If you cannot then play on his outraged manhood with a large order, you should not be a salesman.

If you are asked for details of your product, you have only to hint at the possibility of increased potency, and/or the preservation of Renaissance canvasses. Get your order signed and move on to

FRANCE

Ah, the French! This race so indomitably urbane, this example of humanity which knows no bounds to the possibility of ultimate improvement, which admits no theoretical hindrance to the limitless soaring of the human spirit, this nation which actually talks this sort of meaningless rubbish given a fraction of the chance.

Luckily, they have one Achilles heel. They are a sucker for the idea of the English upper class in a way which the English lower classes have long since learnt to resist. All you have to do is suggest that your product produces a spray-on Milord effect, and you are home and quick-drying. The scent of English lawns . . . the soft embrace of Scottish tweeds . . . the gentle touch of fox-hounds . . . the misty appeal of Wellington boots . . . the old-fashioned flavour of public school floggings . . . That's what the Froggies are after.

Plus, of course, a hint that during the war you suffered dreadfully from . . .

GERMANY

Where you can safely drop a hint that if only England and Germany had been on the same side, things would have been over by 1942. Because if there's one marketing zone in Europe which resembles England, it's Germany, with the same emphasis on pragmatic virtues, hard-headed experience and practical knowledge of the world. What makes it difficult to admit this, naturally, is that Germany has made much better use of such qualities in the last twenty-five years, and we have tended only to pay lip service to them.

Nevertheless, lip service can be a trump card. Thanks to the Americans, English is now the language of international commerce, and you can sway the Germans by explaining to them that your product is . . .

Ein Tip-Top Spray-On Produkt . . .

Das Super Long-Term Aerosol Effekt . . .

Der Wunder-Trendy Skin-Food . . .

Ein Anti-Sovietisches Kalorie-Frei Gentlemen's Overkoat . . .

Villagers Can't Be Choosers

by JOHN CROSBY

Our village has to share a curate with Hermitage, another village two miles down the road. In olden days—well, fifty years ago—this village had its very own, 100 per cent home-owned and even home-grown vicar. No more. Now we own only 50 per cent of our curate who rushes back and forth and has been heard to say he sometimes doesn't know whether he's here or there.

That's what's happening to village life in England in 1973. You share things with other villages. This village once had three shops, including a picturesque Ye Quainte Olde One at the bend at the head of our street. It burned down and was replaced by a wider bend in the road. That's the trend in villages—fewer shops and wider bends on the roads. There were two shops when we moved here six years ago. Now there's only one and it has changed hands twice since we've been here, alas.

Our village once had its own railroad station (you could get on to a sleeping car and not change till Edinburgh, they say), its very own policeman (we share a constable who is known as Sergeant Pepper with three other villages now), its own nurse (you have to go clear to Newbury to caress a real live nurse these days), and its own blacksmith. (What's a blacksmith, Daddy?) What's left? Well, we have our own church (1,000 years old I tell the visitors. Next summer I plan to tell them 1,200 years old, examining their faces for traces of credulity), our very own cemetery (I plan to be buried in it. I tell my wife to avoid the expense of a hearse and use the wheelbarrow since it's only forty yards away), a school, and a garage. It's not as beautiful as some but on frosty mornings when mist shrouds the cemetery and sun is on the encircling hills it can take your breath away..

History? Well, let's see now. The Romans were here and I like to think they made the outward wall of our garage which looks suspiciously Roman. They dug up a 2,000 year old skeleton of a giant of a man in front of our house and we still have our giants. Mr. Loftey is the tallest bell-ringer in England, and conceivably the biggest beekeeper in the whole world. I point him out to the visitors from the city. "Permanently snow-capped," I say. "His bees can only fly as high as his left elbow."

D. H. Lawrence almost but not quite rented the cottage at the head of our lane. He called our hamlet "a dear little village asleep forever". It's waking up, D.H. We now have a nuclear physicist, which shows which way the wind is blowing. In the old days, our village contained only two sorts of people—vicars and gentlemen farmers. (You didn't count farm labour any more than you counted the cows.) Now, in addition to that nuclear fellow, we have a lady who makes dried flowers that sell like hot cakes to you city slickers, a lady interior decorator (who numbers a Beatle among her customers), a man who sells rare books, a poet, and two novelists (one of them, me). All engaged in cottage industry. In the old days, they bent over their machines until the wee hours, spinning flax, at starvation wages; and today they bend over their machines until the wee hours, spinning fiction, at starvation wages. Progress.

Asleep? My goodness, D.H., there is more passionate politics in this village than at Westminster. My wife is on the parish council which is rent at the moment over whether to put the new bus shelter on This Side of the road. Or on That Side. It has been argued with surpassing eloquence that on its way to Reading, the bus stops on This Side. The opposition has replied with thunderous logic that, on its way *back* from Reading, the bus stops on That Side. Impasse. It may take years.

We don't rush into decisions here. The red hot question: should there or should there not be litter baskets on the main street was fought over for two years. (Even to suggest to an Englishman that he should place his litter in a place preordained by other minds was, it was felt, an intolerable violation of his civil rights.) Then there was The Bequest. The lady who owned our house left the church £80 to do as it saw fit. It took two years to decide to use the money to paint the church interior, four years to decide on the colour white and six months to decide which *shade* of white—off-white, oyster, cream.

Democracy at a snail's pace, I call it. But it does have a human face. My wife is incessantly baking things for the senior citizens' Tuesday get-together, or for church socials, or the horticultural society. I'm getting fat just eating the leftovers from all this baking. Since I am an American, the village sniffed at me suspiciously for about three years to be sure they wouldn't catch something awful if they said hello. Now I mingle. I don't of course, occupy high office like my wife who is English. I am generally called on to start things. Well, I started the Shrove Tuesday pancake race, blowing the whistle with and *eclat* not seen in these parts since Cromwell passed through. (Next year I hope we can get a gun to start the race. Whistle, indeed!) I also hand out prizes here and there, the Horticulture Show, things like that. Somebody else reads the names, of course, because no one can understand my thick American accent.

My nationality is very good for openers at cocktail parties. "My cousin lived in Pittsburgh once. She moved away." "It could only happen in America," I agree. Or *this* gambit, which happens all the time: "Visiting, are you?" "No, I live here." "Oh!" What you English can do with that expletive is fairly paralysing. It comes out like *Ee-yeouw* and it expresses disapproval, disdain, despair, all at once.

"*Didn't he do well!*"

Our house is 270 years old and the apple trees were planted personally by Queen Anne, I tell our luncheon guests. Well, you have to tell them something. After all it's a long drive and you must make it worth their while. That's half the fun of living in a village—lording it over the city slickers living in all that pollution. "You mean you have to pay *money* to park your car? What will they think up next?" That's the sort of thing you say to the city dwellers. Or: "What! One pound for lamb's liver! It's one third that much here. What you're paying, dear fellow, is that expensive London ground rent. Out here, of course, we grow all our own lettuce . . . all our vegetables really." (A big lie, but how will they know?)

The London crowd counter weakly with all those museums and concerts they have at their elbow that you know (having lived there) they never go near. Curiously enough you *do* go to museums and the theatre in London a lot when you live in the country, largely I suspect because you have no other place to sit down, after you've given up your flat. The gas strike passed us by. No gas in the village. The electric strike left us unscathed because we have fireplaces and cook on a coal stove. And of course there's all that fresh air. Our air is so fresh city folk swoon dead away. Oxygen poisoning.

I love village life, largely I suspect because I have had my fill of the glamour and tumult of cities. (I've lived in New York, Paris, London, San Francisco.) But that fellow over there lounging by the bus shelter would tell you a quite different story. He's not waiting to get on the bus; he's just waiting to see who gets on the bus. Or who gets off. Because that's the most exciting thing to do in this village. He was born here—and he can't wait to get out of the place.

And when—and if—he does get out then *you* can buy the little house his parents bought in 1935 for £600 for as little as £30,000. And after you buy it you can spend another £15,000 putting in hot water, electricity, oil fired furnaces and all those citified things you're trying to get away from.

58   *"And for my next trick I wonder if I may have the assistance of a member of the audience?"*

Warmest thanks
to ANDRE PREVIN
for these kind words
on

GRATITUDE

I have, in the course of my career, been subject to many interviews, not because my opinions on music and life are so vital to the curriculum of the reader, but because my profession often takes me to cities in which the biggest event of the day is otherwise curtailed to a new census of the canine population, or gossip collected at the barber shop. Inevitably, one of the standard questions raised by the lady journalists of, say, Akron, Ohio (they are always ladies), is "to whom are you grateful, Maestro, who has had the most influence on your life?"

I usually manage to blush prettily and stammer out the expected drivel about teachers, idols, and parents, totally to the satisfaction of the local Medusa, but these are not the real answers. As a result of *Punch's* invitation to contribute some thoughts on this very same subject, I have subjected myself to pitiless scrutiny and have come up with the following verities.

My first thank-you letter must be posted to Adolf Hitler, address somewhere in Argentina. I was born in Berlin and was attending the Konservatorium there, when my father took exception to such lovable signposts as "No Jews Or Bicyclists Allowed In The Park", and decided we should get the hell out. The fact that this decision meant the uprooting of everything he owned and had worked for, and that our leave-taking was crammed with the ingredients of a cheap thriller, border crossings and all, meant very little to me at the time.

I was a very small child and thought it a great adventure. With hindsight, however, it occurs to me that if it hadn't been for Adolf's carpet chewing, I very likely would now be either a rehearsal pianist at the Opera House in Kassel, teaching fat sopranos "The Caliph of Baghdad", or a music professor in Bavaria. So, lots of gratitude, dear Adolf, sent air mail express, but mind where you open the envelope.

Next on my list is Lassie, the beloved collie star. This needs a bit of exposition. The tides of 1940 carried my family and me to the United States, and subsequently to California. There, driven by equal amounts of necessity and greed, I put my musical knowledge to work in the beehives of Hollywood, along with the other drones. I did well, by the local standards. I collected enough awards and statuettes to fetch, at least, four dollars at any pawn shop in the western world, and was as highly respected as any composer can be in the land of perpetual orange juice. One day I was sitting in a producer's office, together with three actors, a starlet (soi-disant), a director, and an executive.

Suddenly, the door opened, and in walked Lassie, accompanied by her owner-trainer, Mr. Rudd Weatherwax. There were the usual heartfelt obsequious Hellos, and then Lassie made the rounds of the room, solemnly sitting up in front of each of the assembled luminaries and offering a languid paw to be shaken, or kissed.

I was beguiled, until she had done her trick seven times, and ambled to my chair. She took one quick look, and with the performer's instinct that comes only after years of treading the boards, recognised I was merely a composer. Her lip curled a bit, she passed me by and floated out, wafted on her way by admiring cries of "what a great star," and "smartest actress of the lot." I must admit that I was shaken. To be snubbed by Darryl Zanuck—well, of course; by Mamie Van Doren—well, naturally. But by a sheep dog? I took it big, I took it hard. I packed and left town very soon after. Darling Lassie, a big bone to you, and may you always do composers and writers the favour of peeing on them.

Conducting a symphony orchestra can have an enormous pitfall; that of misplaced feelings of power and knowledge. Since my tenure with the London Symphony Orchestra began, five years ago, I have had occasion to be grateful to quite a few people for reminding me, gently or otherwise, not to take myself too seriously. I remember working with Wilhelm Kempff, the great German pianist, whose performances are usually described by the critics as "magisterial". Herr Kempff was in his late seventies at the time of our concert together, and he was playing the Schumann Concerto. We were standing in the wings of the Festival Hall, ready to go on, when I said to him, "You must have played this piece hundreds of times. Can you remember the very first time?" Kempff smiled at my attempts at small talk. "Oh yes, young man," he answered, "I remember particularly well." The door opened and we walked out onto the stage. As the applause began, I continued, determined to be sophisticatedly calm. "Can you remember who was conducting?" The old gentleman looked benign, and threw the knife. "Debussy," he said, and suddenly I felt eighteen inches tall.

On another occasion, I was sent to conduct a provincial Italian orchestra. I had had several years of impeccable playing in my ears, courtesy of the LSO and other great orchestras, and was totally unprepared for the work awaiting me. The Turin players behaved like butterfly collectors; they sneaked up on each bar, and then desperately clapped a net over it. They viewed tempi the same way they drove their Fiats, fast during solo stretches, and insane in heavy traffic. They were sweet and kind, but bewildered that I might want things a bit more orderly. My admonitions were, by necessity, sketchy.

My Italian is limited to ordering the wrong food in Soho, and the orchestra's English consisted of rapid hand movements, eye rollings, and muttered imprecations. At one point, a fight broke out in the percussion section, of such vehemence that I thought I was witnessing the denouement of an ancient Sicilian vendetta, only to have the two protagonists come up to the rostrum, arm in arm, and explain that the altercation had been about whose turn it was to move the bass drum into place. Heartfelt gratitude, Signori, for reminding me that a conductor is as good as the orchestra in front of him.

We were playing Fairfield Hall, in Croydon, recently. Around the back is the small parking lot reserved for the performers. I drove my Volkswagen Camper through the special barrier, and swung it smartly into the space

"Gosh, I'm so corrupt, and you're really swell to take it the way you do."

"Maybe you'd care to take it and read it at home?"

labelled "reserved for conductor". I was fishing out my scores, baton case, and clothing bag, all of which had been lost in the back seat morass of my twins' necessities of life, such as biscuits, a tricycle, and a rocking duck, when the commissionaire sprinted up, wattles aflame.

"What do you think you're doing in that space, mate?" he demanded.

"I'm the conductor," I answered securely, brandishing my copy of Beethoven's Seventh.

"Oh come now," the voice was dripping with sarcasm, "if you're the conductor, where's your driver?"

Where, indeed? and where, while we're at it, is my Rolls Royce, my private railway car, my gold cigarette case, my nubile Girl Friday, my knowledge of wines, and my impeccable wardrobe? As a matter of fact, where are the keys to my Volkswagen Camper? Could someone please give me directions home? I'd be so grateful!

The Punch Diet Sheet for Those Who Can't Afford to Eat

Food is running short . . . prices are rising . . . meat getting rarer . . . so now is the time to go on the world's first glamorous course that actually lets you slim as you save . . .

Dieticians have recently discovered that many of the foods which are reputedly good for health and conducive to slimmer, more beautiful bodies, actually contain harmful **high prices.** A fillet steak, for instance, which is low on calories and high on protein, undoes all its good work by its enormous content of **aggregate cost** (a technical term for the loss of £'s involved). It may even render the eater unable to have another good meal for 24 hours.

Another alarming discovery is that many hitherto reputable foods are subject to **reduced availability.** This is a highly complicated scientific concept, but roughly it means that if **Vogue** recommended all its readers to eat quail to make their cheeks soft, and all the readers took the advice, the quail would become extinct overnight. As any ecologist will tell you, this would alter the shape of the Scottish landscape radically, as well as make the ptarmigan feel nervous.

The answer we have devised is quite simple. Eat foods which are low on **income damage.** Choose dishes which have a maximum **re-use value.** That way you will be able to eat as much as you like—as long as you keep strictly to this seven-day diet chart! (To begin with, many of you will find it difficult to restrict yourselves to **cost-free** foods. You're bound to lapse now and again, but persevere; the temptation to change a pound note will soon vanish. Remember, it's always better to save than slim.)

DAY 1
breakfast
half a grapefruit
small cup of coffee
Any type of grapefruit would do, but the best kind is the one that rolls by accident off the greengrocer's stall into your shopping bag. Eat the segments, but do not squeeze. *No sugar and milk in your coffee.* Sugar and milk are full of dangerous *cost escalation.*

lunch
half a grapefruit

small cup of coffee
The other half of breakfast's grapefruit—again do not squeeze. For a change, try your cup of coffee iced. This avoids harmful hidden *heating charges*.

dinner
grapefruit juice
snoek and knödel pie
cheese
Squeeze the two grapefruit halves left over from breakfast and lunch. Snoek and knödel pie is cooked in exactly the same way as steak and kidney pie, except that snoek is used instead of steak and knödel instead of kidneys. Knödel are German dumplings, which are made by letting lumps of pastry fall into the pie. This dish is traditionally eaten with the fingers, which avoids unnecessary *cutlery investment*. For cheese, why not try one of the wide range of English offerings such as mouse-trap (available in most good mouse-traps)?

DAY 2
breakfast
Scottish rarebit
small cup of coffee
Scottish rarebit is a variant of the more familiar Welsh rarebit, made with dust instead of cheese. Just pop a piece of toast under the grill for a moment and it's ready.

lunch
oeuf cuit a l'eau bouillant
A satisfying French regional dish, made by leaving an egg in boiling water for four minutes. If this is too rich for your taste, leave the egg for dinner and skip lunch.

supper
hard-boiled egg
scrag end of loaf
For the main dish, ask your baker to carve you off a crusty joint—the so-called Door-Step. It can be toasted, grilled or barbecued; whichever way you prepare it, these lesser-known cuts have unexpected *investment value*.

DAY 3
breakfast
nothing

lunch
nothing

dinner
crab ramekins
gigot d'agneau, with carrots, artichokes and salsify
syllabub
choice of seven cheeses
brandy
The best recipe for this deeply satisfying meal is being invited out to dinner. If you have it at home it is not at all satisfying—try half a grapefruit for a change.

DAY 4
breakfast
roast half of grapefruit
champignon sur pain grillé
The mushroom dish, a perennial favourite with impoverished old ladies in Provence, consists of a single mushroom diced and lightly fried in its own dripping, placed on a soupçon of toast.

lunch
mackerel, Viennese style
The Viennese do not like mackerel. Sensibly, they much prefer the cheaper cuts of whitebait.

dinner
potage mackerel, Viennese style
casserole de potage mackerel, Viennese style
bread et marge pudding

DAY 5
breakfast
oeuf sans saucisse, lard, tomate et champignons

lunch
pensioner's rabbit pie
Pensioners have traditionally found rabbit too rich a dish, and have long preferred to replace it with hamster which can be obtained free from any pet shop/primary school. Is traditionally served with no vegetables.

dinner
rolled joint
Obtainable locally

DAY 6
breakfast
cocktail de supreme de left-over de

grapefruit
toast a la maison

lunch
veal escalope milanese a la muggeridge
The celebrated chef Muggeridge based this recipe on a report in some newspaper or other that calves received unutterably cruel treatment while in transit from Rouen to Marseille, and deleted the veal element from the dish. It remains a classic of the *cost-free* pasta school.

dinner
whelk cocktail
lapin bourguignon
crab apple fool

DAY 7
breakfast
large cup of coffee

lunch
viande et deux legumes
A classic French dish based on an old meat and vegetable recipe. Nowadays it takes the form of sauté left-over plus left-overs, though this is usually dropped in favour of a ham sandwich *a la luncheon voucher*.

dinner
lettuce vinaigrette
blackbird pie
zabaglione (optional: to be refused)

JUST GOOD FRIENDS

JOHN CLEESE throws an arm around the first of a new series and leads it gently to the typewriter for a friendly natter

"He's wonderful with children . . ."

I am glad to say that I have a lot of friends including Ian Fordyce (TV Producer), Michael and Helen Fipp's', Nicholas Walt, Mr. Bailey and many others.

I do not need to name them all in this "article" but I have a great deal of them (almost *too* many in fact!) although I pride myself I do not make a fetish about it, like for instance some people make out huge lists of "Friends" and leave them lying around on the coffee table, pretending they had intended to put them in a drawer but had forgotten to do so in the rush, just to rattle you, but I usually find that half the names, if you press the point, turn out to be people they've just asked information from at information bureaus and then copied their names down from the plastic things they have their names printed on which they have on the counters in front of them when you ask them for the information, or even floor-walkers in Selfridge's and people like that who must have badges pinned to them.

These names get quite easy to spot after a while, for instance if any of your friends' lists have "E. W. Newell" on them, he is the man who gives information at King's Cross and "Miss B. Sagar" was the lady in charge of Soft Toys at Derry and Toms before they closed. I actually know someone who once saw the name of the Fortnum and Mason Pie Department Assistant Manager on the friend-list of a famous Station Master! And he doesn't even wear a badge so he must have looked him up in *Who's Who* or somewhere!

Incidentally, if any of you spot names on your friends' lists that look suspect I can easily check them for you. I could find out and then you could come round to dinner if you were free, any time really, I'm usually in, and I could

"I think it's cruel the way they keep them cooped up in those little cages."

give you the details. You could leave when you wanted to, I'm not one of those people who get nasty when you want to go a bit early because you have to be up in the morning. I mean, just for an example, suppose the conversation *has* finally died, or the veal-and-ham *was* a bit off, it's always better to accept the rebuff gracefully, I always say, and show your guest out with a smile, than get involved in a scuffle with him. Not that it's ever been a problem with me but I've seen people lose more, well, *potential* friends by oversensitivity in the early stages than by anything except strong religious feelings. Anyway do think it over, there's always room for one more!

Anyway, as I was saying, I believe that one's friend-list should only include one's real friends and acquaintances, for example, I could easily have written down Malcolm Kerr but I haven't seen him for quite a bit and I don't think it's really fair to say someone's a friend if you haven't seen them for *that* long, although he is really. I don't think you should include *anyone* you haven't seen for, say ten years, *unless* they've been away and only then really if they've written at least once. (Unless things have been absolutely hectic for them.) And also you shouldn't put down people either who were friends once but definitely aren't any more. Mr. Bailey does this, although he admittedly puts them under a special heading, but I say this is cheating although the Fipp's' think it's O.K. if you make it clear that they're not *good* friends. Well! That makes the whole *point* of the thing ridiculous. I mean *I* haven't put down Alan Hutchison, although he was my best friend until May 22nd last year, because you can't call somebody *any* variety of friend after you've had a scrap as prolonged as ours, particularly when it was his fault to start with. I

mean we'd always got on very well, because we had the same number of friends on our lists. (Or very nearly, he always had one or two more than me but it's stupid harbouring a grudge about a small difference like that.)

But then *when* we agreed to pool all our friends, which was a brilliant idea because we both doubled our total, but which was *his* idea, I discovered, *after* the whole deal was finished and the agreement signed (and witnessed by Mr. Bailey), that over half of his list (3 out of 5) were actually dead! He'd not even copied them out of the street directory, he'd just taken them off tombstones! So he'd gained six real ones from me (or five anyway because I admit Sir Alf Ramsey was debatable) while I'd only got two from him, so that from really being 5-2 down he was now 7 all. He'd tricked me all along so that he could do the deal and get level.

I mean if he'd taken them out of the street directory I'd have spotted it eventually because you get to know those names after you've been at it a few years, but off *graves!* I honestly never thought anyone could stoop to that, and I said so, quite straight, and then he said that *my* friends might just as well be dead for all the use they were to anyone, and I asked him what he meant by that, and he said they were disturbed to a man, and that even Mr. Bailey, who was once a teacher, had written the wrong name down when we asked him to sign the agreement, and that the Fipp's' were after me for what they could get, and that it was Nicholas Walt who had trodden on my hamster (to get even with me for my accident with his) and not the gas-man, and I said the Fipp's' were a charming couple, and he said what about the suggestions they had made to me, and I said that while I did not fully concur with all their views about the physical side of friendship, the essence of true companionship was the toleration of views abhorrent to oneself, and that Nicholas was *not* a spiteful man (though actually he is) (it had never occurred to me about Winston but it had the ring of truth) and, I said, what about Mr. Fordyce, my TV producer friend, who directed many dramas we had all watched together at my place, and Alan said that he had emigrated in 1967 and had asked him not to tell me where.

This was a lie actually, but I fell for it because we *had* been out of touch, and so, to cut a long story short, an awful fracas took place. Anyway I'll tell you all the details when you come round for a bite to eat, next week is good for me, most weeks are O.K. actually, just drop in any time really, except I usually go for a bit of a walk about 3 a.m.

So see you next week if you can make it, and you can go when you want, as I said. Incidentally if Malcolm Kerr reads this do give me a call, I'd love a cup of tea, even a game of squash. I've improved a lot since the last time we played.

66

On the eve of Britain's sending a sales team to China for the Spring Trade Fair, PICTURE-PROBE went out behind the bamboo curtain to ask:

Will the Chinaman in the Street be Buying British?

Enjoying a long, cool smoke in his lunch minute was Hsi Chiao Nim, 102, from Shanghai, who works at The People's Dispensary for Household Bauxite, Paraffin, Mica Scrap, Oil Cakes, Malleable Bones and Essential Medicinal Herbs, where he sweeps up. He has no fixed plans to take up an option on Concorde, he claims, but would like to see the new range of Marks & Spencer cotton polyester overalls.

Waiting for a bus by a telephone pole was short-sighted Ng Fung Kou, a father of 88 from Tientsin, who is a peasant and works in cereals. He would like very much to see a London double-decker bus or for that matter a single-decker Chinese one or even a humble ox-cart which could give him a lift back home to Tientsin. He'd bought a Beefeater Automatic Brolly from the fair, mistaking it for a rolling pin.

A tense moment for would-be British exporters as Liao Fang Pei, Teck Soon and Men Wai Shih, executives from the Chinese State Trading Corporation, experiment playing Peking chess with authentic Pontefract cakes. A world famine of quality liquorice is feared if there's an order from China, which may use them also as novelty buttons.

The population explosion in China, which has clearly taken the beachwear and seaside novelties industry by surprise, also made for a disappointing start to this year's Kowloon People's Regatta, as our picture shows. Few, if any, of the home-built sculling boats, traditionally fashioned from human hair and bamboo, met the specification, leaving these semi-finalists to jostle for position in the turbulent Yangtse-Kiang. None of the citizens shown was even on the waiting-list for an XJ6 and fewer than one in six million had heard of Jimmy Young.

Kwangchow housewife Hu Shou Po, pictured in a busy Canton shopping street with her grandson, Ngo, works as a part-time People's Counsellor on seeds, but has no strong views on whether the VC10 production line should be re-opened. She feels that there may well be a brisk market for underwear for Ngo, who feels the cold.

"What a knockout! Nelson Eddy and Janet MacDonald in one package!"

The Gay Seventies

by HEATH

"Of course, I can remember when you could laugh at poofs in the street for nothing."

"I bet it is—shaving
nine times a day."

"Look, Dave, if you want to stay with the group, you're going to
have to pull yourself together!"

"Nobody loves you when you're old
and gay."

"No, actually I'm the male lead—it's only
offstage I'm in drag."

...AND NOW THE

NATIONWIDE
DAY OFF
CHAOS
CAUSED
BY RAIL
STRIKE

Dickinson

Depressed by the papers?
Suicidal after the 9 o'clock bulletin?
Convinced the world is ending?

Of course you are. That's because, like most people, you think crisis talk and strike reports are *bad* news. Nothing of the sort! Approached in the right way, even the worst headlines can yield untold happiness and optimism. It simply requires a new orientation to life, which can be reached after a few simple exercises. All you need is a copy of the *Daily Telegraph*, a comfortable chair and a bottle of champagne. Now you're ready to begin...

EXERCISE ONE

Find the most "depressing" headline you can. Say, for instance, "ONE DAY RAIL STRIKE THROWS NATION INTO CHAOS". Normally you would look at it and pass on, feeling depressed. This time sit back and think about it. Then write down on a piece of paper what it means.

   i.   The railways have stopped working for a day.

   ii. Many people have not been able to get to work.

   iii. Production in some areas has been halted for a few hours. That doesn't seem quite so bad, does it? Not exactly what you would call chaotic, anyway. Perhaps that headline should have read: "ONE DAY RAIL STRIKE PUTS NATION TO INCONVENIENCE". Perhaps there should have been a photograph of railway workers at home, planting their wallflowers. Picture a railwayman at home, planting his wallflowers. What colour do you like wallflowers?

By exercise seven you will be ready to say "ONE DAY RAIL STRIKE PROMOTES WALLFLOWER GROWTH", but that will take practice. Meanwhile, master these simple phrases.

"Britain is actually in a period of unparalleled economic growth."

"Flying is by far the safest method of air travel."

"French phones are terrible."

GOOD NEWS!!

EXERCISE TWO

Don't take our word for it. *Phone* somebody in France. Just try. All you have to do is dial twenty-six (vingt-six) digits and put cream on your blisters. Remember, of course, that Continental phone signals are completely different from ours. A rapidly repeated pip means the number is engaged. A far-off skirling noise means that you forgot the fifteenth digit. Busy static is a sign that your call has been re-routed to Lucerne.

It is just possible that you may be answered by a voice saying "Allo?", which means that you have got through to your friend in France. Do not be dismayed. Think of it as an example of the marvellous way we can instantly get through to our friends in France, because the secret of enjoying the news is in realising that *somebody always benefits*.

That is why the sports pages are so popular. There is always a winner. When a draw results, there are *two* winners. *You* can use this method for political news as well, as in "ONE DAY RAIL STRIKERS RUN OUT WORTHY WINNERS IN CLOSE CONTEST", or "RAILMEN DO WELL IN ONE DAY WATERLOO EVENT".

A few more phrases, now :—

"Poor old dollar."

"At last we have a leader who isn't afraid to change his mind."

"I, personally, was not involved in an air crash of any kind today."

"Did you read that they have invented the non-stick sausage?"

EXERCISE THREE

Limber up with a few more headlines. Take the worst you can find and feel happy for the beneficiaries. "CHAOS AS SNOW SWEEPS ENGLAND" will make a few million children happy. "GRIM PROSPECT FOR CAR INDUSTRY" means, of course, emptier roads and fewer crashes. "BRITAIN'S SPRING TRADE FIGURES WILL BE BLEAK" should arouse the thought: But not for the Japanese. (Ideally, one should not try to bring foreigners into this— later, you will simply react by thinking: "Good, it's almost almond blossom time".) "AIR CRASH: 76 DEAD" can simply be met with satisfied thoughts of the air traffic control improvements this is bound to bring. (Advanced students may care to try: "A much-needed shot in the arm for the salvage industry".)

Remember that this system has nothing to do with the idea of looking for good, positive news, that has been put around recently. *To go looking for happy headlines is a counsel of despair.* Our motto is "Every cloud has a load of much needed rain".

Think about that one day rail strike again. How would you translate it now? "RAIL STOPPAGE GIVES NATION DAY OFF"? "RAIL STANDSTILL EASES STRESS PROBLEMS EVERYWHERE"?

Two more handy phrases :—

"Is this a new crisis or a repeat of an old one?"

"I'm all for property developers, now that they have started to demolish hideous modern buildings."

EXERCISE FOUR

Try going without papers or TV news for a few days. If you have been doing your exercises properly, *this should leave you depressed,* because you have been deprived of headlines to see the bright side of.

EXERCISE FIVE

Sooner or later you will meet a headline which seems to leave everyone the loser. For instance, "BRITAIN FACES WATER CRISIS IN FIFTEEN YEARS". Even the most advanced student won't get much fun out of feeling happy for cactus growers and camel owners. The secret here is to read on till you find a *fascinating statistic*. In this case it is almost certain to be "Each of us uses 50 gallons of water a day." "50 gallons?" you say to yourself. "*I* don't. Well, I suppose a bath uses up a few gallons, but I don't always have a big bath. Don't always have a bath, come to that. On the other hand, they may be adding on to my score some of the water the guy next door wastes on his car and a few of the gallons Paul Getty puts in his swimming pool. I wonder what a gallon looks like? Wonder if Paul Getty has a pool?"

This sort of idle speculation does wonders for any insoluble headline—by the time you've got round to visualising Paul Getty doing the breast stroke, Britain's water crisis is far away.

Now test yourself. How would you react to these headlines?

"EARTH'S FUEL SUPPLIES MAY NOT OUTLAST CENTURY."

"EARTH CANNOT FEED ITSELF, SAYS SCIENTIST."

EXERCISE SIX

By now you should be able to enjoy even the grimmest headline, and it will be child's play to mutter to yourself, "Another two millions people not shot in Northern Ireland today" or "This is one of the classic fuel crises of our times— an authentic masterpiece".

But there is a danger to look out for. It is impossible to avoid coming across the occasional totally cheerful headline. Your training will now tempt you to start automatically looking for the black side of the news. If the newsman says beamingly: "Something for everybody in today's Budget," you will find it hard not to mutter "And nothing much for anybody". Fight against it. Tell yourself that things might really be as good as they say they are.

How's that one day rail strike coming along? Have you discovered Betjeman's Law yet? "DESERTED LONDON TERMINI PRESENT UNIQUE CHANCE TO VIEW VICTORIAN RAILWAY ARCHITECTURE".

Above all, keep practising. On Tuesdays and Thursdays, think of Jeremy Thorpe as Leader of the Opposition. Set aside fifteen minutes each day for seeing Heath v. the unions as the thrilling sight of democracy in action.

EXERCISE SEVEN

If you've worked hard, you should be ready now for the final test which will make you a fully qualified happy newsreader. If you react properly to this last news item, you will never need to refer to these two pages again. Ready?

"*PUNCH* WORSENS NATIONAL CRISIS WITH IRRESPONSIBLE ARTICLE URGING ESCAPIST ATTITUDE TO NEWS."

"Doris, love—everyone went home ages ago."

Father of the Groom

By KEITH WATERHOUSE

The wedding has taken place at St. George's Church, Hanover Square, between Miss Emma Jane Fourfeathers, only daughter of Sir Douglas and Lady Fourfeathers, and Mr. Terry Spratt, eldest son of Mr. Ron Spratt, windows cleaned, no job too small or too big, our quotation no obligation, and Mrs. Spratt. After a reception held at the Ritz Hotel, the following notes fell from the lifeless fingers of Mr. Spratt as he was helped into the police van.

Lords, ladies, gentleman, friends, Lady Fourfeathers, Sir Fourfeathers, one and all. Unaccustomed as am public speaking, feel opportunity should not go by without saying few words. Not often lady wife and self are up West; as for present erotic surroundings, never in born days. Lifetime motto however has always been speak as you find, so as find all and sundry dressed as if for Royal paddock at Ascot race-track, will try and keep speech at same exalted level. Wait for laughter.

Make mention of food and drink served, as it might be sherry, whisky, gin-and-tons, sidecars, vino, champagne, brandy with all the trimmings, chicken vollavongs, caviare on hot toast, trifle, cake, &c &c. Thank catering firm, Messrs. The Ritz. Tell one about Pakki what opens this catsmeat shop, only he had to close it again because he can't get no more cats. Wait for laughter.

Thank Sir and Lady Fourfeathers for graciously condescending to invite self and lady wife here today, also our Terry for at long last telling us where he hid invitation, will not go into that now it will save till him and little Emma Jane get back from their honeymoon on the island of Greece. Seriously though, sincerely grateful Sir Fourfeathers for giving self and lady wife chance see how other half lives.

Sir Fourfeathers is good bloke. Proud to know him. Would like to shake him by hand. Puts self in mind of little story, stop self if heard it, about this woman with no legs and this geezer comes up and gives her one. After it is all over and he has unhooked her off of railings, she thanks him for being real gentleman—all other bleeders have left her hanging up there. Wait for laughter.

Like geezer in story, Sir Fourfeathers is gentleman in every sense of word. Is proper toff. Is definitely all right, have always thought so ever since first met him when our Terry had great misfortune to put little Emma Jane up stick. Have learned a lot more about Sir Fourfeathers since them days. Have learned to respect him. May have dirty great country house also flat in Park Lane, but grafts for living same as self. Is chairman and managing director of fourteen companies, sits on board of umpteen others, also is magistrate, so this your lucky day lads, you can tear up them parking tickets and obstruction summonses.

Now is neither time or place, but man in Sir Fourfeathers' position must often have occasion to review window cleaning contract. Country house alone must have seven hundred burnt cinders (point out this is Cockney rhyming slang for windows), not to mention numerous office blocks. Self can offer competitive quotation at favourable rates. Do not know if our Terry intends stay in family business now he has fallen on feet, but if does, place can always be found for little Emma Jane. Can always write out invoices, brew up tea, sweep floor &c, &c, better than watching telly

"I knew he'd soon get tired of that karate thing."

"I don't like to bother you on such a short acquaintance, Dr. Livingstone, it's probably nothing, but I get this sort of stabbing pain in the chest and . . ."

in Palace Gate while waiting for our Terry to come in off of round. As Sir Fourfeathers now one of family, will tell him what will do. All windows cleaned at 25 per cent off going rate. Cannot say fairer than that.

Thank best man for toasts to bridesmaids. Point out that same include our Marlene and our Sandra. Could not help noticing big number of single men on bride's side of church today—have been told they all stock-brokers, big advertising men, company directors, you name it. While our Marlene nothing write home about as regards looks, has got good head on shoulders and has been to secretarial school so could write up books, make out swindle sheets &c, &c, in short would be asset. Is good plain cook. Squint could be put right if necessary funds forthcoming. As for our Sandra, is supposed to be engaged to mate of our Terry's but this can always be got out of. As self has always told her, marry a bleeding barrow boy and you won't go no further in life, you have got to look after number one, why not wait for Mr. Right and have own big house, big car &c &c. So our Marlene and our Sandra both definitely available, get in there lads what are you waiting for.

Tell one about this bloke who goes to doctor and says doctor doctor, am getting married and do not know how to go about it. Doctor says, just put hand on her belly and say I love you. So, bloke gets married, goes on honeymoon, puts hand on bird's belly and say I love you. Bird says, lower, lower. So bloke says (put on low voice), I love you. Wait for laughter.

This brings self to subject of our Terry and little Emma Jane. Not losing son, gaining daughter is way self looks at it. May all troubles be little ones. Wish them all would wish selves, if as happy as self and self's old

74

dutch, cannot go far wrong. Will not presume offer them no advice, they could teach self also Sir and Lady Fourfeathers thing or two if you was to ask self. All will say is, hope bed-springs at Ritz Hotel also on island of Greece is in better nick than them at No. 4 Peterloo Buildings, talk about creak creak creak, self is only surprised that never had bleeding ceiling down. If got time, tell one about dog chucking bucket of water over this honeymoon couple. Wait for laughter. Ask Lady Fourfeathers if she gets it. If she says no, say why not, don't tell self Sir Fourfeathers is past it.

Last but not least, would like to scotch rumour that our Terry was after little Emma Jane for what could get. May have put her in pod, has never denied it, but was not first pig in trough by long chalk. Could mention certain guards officer, no names no pack drill, also certain young geezer here today, cannot pick him out, all look same in evening dress, like bleeding penguins. Also not true he went sniffing round her for her money. Did not know she had all that much, thought at first she was high-class Mayfair tart. Anyway, why she hanging about in Hackney boozer if not looking for rough trade, she wanted him now she has got him.

Still, all that water under bridge. Would once again thank Sir Money-bags, beg his pardon, Sir Fourfeathers, for sit-down nosh-up, would ask all present to be upstanding, if so capable at this stage—wait for laughter—and drink second toast to our Terry and little Emma Jane, this time coupled with name of little stranger. Wait for applause. Tell one about Jewish doctor and bloke with no nose. Do imitation of blind man drinking cup of tea. Pick up wedding cake and ask Lady Fourfeathers if she would like a bit. If she says yes, say why, is Sir Fourfeathers keeping you short of it?

"It's pollution but of a rather high order."

Christmas v. the Environment

by THELWELL

"I insisted on it being free-range."

"Save your breath. They've had the place sound-proofed."

"Are you going to feel guilty all Christmas again?"

"There doesn't seem very much wrong with the quality of life."

"We must be above the tree-line."

"Grubbing out all the hedges! There's hardly a bit of holly to be had."

"Martha! The dust men have left us a tip."

MY NEXT HUSBAND

by Jacky Gillott

There will be no next husband. Should the present holder of the post by some sorry chance pass over (more probably *under* something), my chances of a second marriage are slight. I'm not saying I'm undesirable, though plenty of other people do, observing how I have let myself go in my land-girl's hand-me-downs. No, it's marriage itself that all self-respecting modern women declare is undesirable and if I'm to go on pretending to be a self-respecting modern woman I want to avoid that easily imagined altar-piece where the vicar, asking why these two might not be conjoined, is faced with Germaine Tweedie listing 374 angrily intelligent reasons against a submission on the part of the woman.

But let me be honest. I am, at bottom (never mind anywhere else), an old-fashioned thing, well able to see that at 87, it might not be a lover I need so much as a friend with whom I can recklessly spend the pension. Still, that said, there remain powerful grounds for supposing I'll never find myself a second husband. First of all there is my first husband, who is indestructible. In spite of a daily habit of hitting his head on something however improbably placed, he has so far survived deportation at gunpoint, any number of armed street brawls in which he had (out of a sense of justice rather than *common*-sense) involved himself, three bouts of malaria and amoebic dysentery, a pudding made out of monkey, alcohol fermented with spit, physical attack by a wild stallion, detention in an Ethiopian leprosarium, public school and ten years of marriage to myself.

Apart from being indestructible, he is—even more importantly—irreplaceable. No, I'm not just being soppy. A glance through the list of requirements I would demand of the next applicant *(should* the situation fall vacant), and the meaning of "irreplaceable" becomes startlingly clear. Clearly unsentimental.

My next husband must laugh readily at all my jokes. He must have the perception to see that beneath my wellingtons, an old woolly vest and three jumpers smelling strongly of horse, there lurks a sexually attractive creature.

At a more routine level, he will abhor the fried breakfast—indeed, any breakfast beyond coffee in quart mugs. He will, to go even further, survive cheerfully on one substantial meal a day.

On the whole question of food—or to re-phrase that, on the question of *whole*food—he will be capable of baking grainy brown loaves that tend towards a slight sogginess in the middle, be gifted in the pickling of onions to a spiciness undreamed-of in shop jars, and be prepared to scrub his own artichokes if he must be addicted to artichoke soup. (Those not strangers to it, will know the soup is identified a long way off by the scent of old, boiled feet.)

The applicant will be expected to grow a rotation of vegetables that lasts all year round, know exactly when to prune, graft, pot and re-pot and be happy to have his heavier labours watched by someone in a deckchair and a bikini. He will mow a great deal of grass, recognise at once which fungi are edible and which are not, know how to deal with rabbit-lice and the tapeworm in cats and continue to love my cats when they scratch up his seedlings. He will arrange flowers in a vase rather better than I do, take his shirts to the laundry and replace his (and his son's) buttons, as and when they drop off.

To put the more malicious reader's imagination at rest, let me make it plain that I am not idling away my time either. All this activity frees me to get on with the mucking-out, think up a few more jokes, fashion a few finely-wrought sentences and, quite frequently, be ill.

As one of God's creatures carefully selected for bruising, dislocation and mysterious virus, I am bound to look for basic nursing skills in my next husband. At least once a week he will have to wash my surgical corset and dry it out overnight so that I can be safely làced back into it the following morning. (I cannot take it off to wash it as, when I *do* take it off, I fall down.) Would my next husband I wonder, after three months of married life, be prepared to work nights so that he could nurse me during the day? And by nurse, I mean bedpans, the lot . . . you can't tell me anything about the new and real intimacy between young people.

He will have other strains to endure. My work, for example.

I shall want him to tiptoe round the house playing I Spy in whispers with the children whilst I apply myself to the great novel. And when *I* decide the great novel is a work of incomparable rubbish, I will need all the sympathy and encouragement he can find it in his heart to give.

As for *his* work, he must be involved in something that gives him plenty of opportunity to get out of the house, to do with travel, with the excitement of new people, new places. Something to balance the astonishing dullness of his home. life.

Television is the ideal job. Only a man who works in television could watch as much of it as our life requires and enjoy the professional, critical pleasure of jeering at some ill-done thing we'd be far better occupied not watching at all.

He will come home with a tan and tales of adventure so bizarre and horrendous, that the staggeringly monotonous routine of his domestic life will seem a welcome haven of peace. Since my present husband has already been the first white man to set foot in the last remaining places, my second husband will need to lie vividly. I used to think my present husband lied (some people still do, one can tell by the glaucous veil over their eyes) but no, all the tales are true, even the one about halting the witch doctor in full froth by dropping on one knee and taking hurried snaps of him.

Yes, gardening, mending and cooking will seem to him like the sweetest relation after his struggles in the jungle. He will be *glad* that I am allergic to parties—whereas some people are sick after an evening's social eating and drinking, I am sick *before* at the very idea of it. He will certainly be too weary to travel a further 150 miles to see the nearest new film or play.

So far then, a remarkable catalogue of the irreplaceable qualities. Surely though, there are one or two . . . not weaknesses, *foibles* perhaps, I would willingly forgo? "I know what you'll say," said my present husband sourly, on hearing the typewriter, ". . . You'll say you're on the look-out for someone two inches taller." "Not at all," I promised him loyally. But since *he* brought the matter up, there are one or two really very, very minor, changes . . . I would so enjoy a gossip. Someone interested enough in scandal to note and report it. Dear God, simply *remember* it. I'd give a lot, heaven knows, for a husband whose dominant gene (it has appeared in both children) was not chronic loss of memory allied to unpredictable, psychological deafness. Dependent as I am on him for news of the outside world (and by news I mean the more scurrilous of current affairs). I am shockingly out of touch on whom is whose.

Besides which, it can be embarrassing to be married to someone unable to introduce you to a third party (always supposing he has not forgotten the appointment he had with the third party) because he can't remember your name.

But there, it's a small thing, nothing to harp upon. After all, it might be said that the last thing needed by a man who can cook, mend and manage flowers to the high standard I would require, is a wife. And that happily, is a question my present husband has forgotten ever to put to himself.

The stunningly beautiful JACKY GILLOTT is a novelist and broadcaster who lives in Somerset. She is married to a BBC producer who is unfortunately very strong.

"Oh no—don't tell me—a back street vasectomist!"

by ALAN COREN

NOW it comes on the spring of 1973, after a long hard winter, and times are very tough indeed, what with the stock market going all to pieces, and sterling creeping around like your cousin with the hernia from Boston, Lincs, and the sidewalks of this city turning out to be paved with stone, and pretty low-grade stone, at that, and many citizens of the area are compelled to do the best they can.

There is very little scratch anywhere, and along Fleet Street many citizens are wearing their last year's clothes, and where you used to see gold watches there is only an empty space, and many prominent hacks on many prominent broadsheets are having to drop in at the hockshop to inquire whether there is still time to get one on for the three-thirty. I personally am carrying my kid's Mickey Mouse alarm clock, which is causing much embarrassment around and about, as it is most cheap and goes off on buses.

So I am not surprised to hear rumours that William the Editor, who is a citizen

that gets very unhappy walking about in plimsolls and his Uncle Louie's second-best overcoat, is planning a way out of these financial extremities. He is a citizen well-known around and about for his monetary acumen, so it is not so strange when he asks me to step in to his office one day last week.

"Things is pretty rough all over, Big Al", he tells me, "so I have been sitting up with the ice-bag and the *Financial Times* and what I have come up with is as follows: there are a number of four-legged items competing at Newmarket this Tuesday, and according to the *Financial Times* and other sources in the know, they are constituting an unbeatable investment. Why, many newspapers are giving us the winners in advance! All we do is go down there with a sack."

I try to explain to William the Editor that these winners are somewhat hypothetical, being based on certain assumptions such as one of the other runners does not come past the post in front of them, but he is new to the Sport of Kings and very excited to discover about such citizens as bookmakers which someone has told him carry the stuff around in suitcases and give it away to deserving causes.

Thus it transpires that on the morning of the aforementioned Tuesday, some thirty citizens of the neighbourhood are standing about in the immediate environs

of the Punch building, looking somewhat secondhand on account of it is not every day of the week that they are vertical at ten a.m., in fact it is none of them. Also, the company is somewhat unsettled by the presence of a tall personality in a black bowler hat whom nobody recognises, and the only time any of them see a tall personality in a black bowler hat is when the furniture is being carried downstairs on the instructions of the Official Receiver. Fortunately, this particular citizen turns out to be Legal Bresler, who is present in an unofficial capacity, i.e. hoping to turn a fast note or two and thereby keep the wolf from the chambers, like everyone else.

In fact, the only person who is actually carrying a smile around to set off his collar is Welsh Harry, a citizen who has carried off the World's Widest Comic Genius title several years running and is in consequence the focus for many pedestrians who wish to touch the hem of his garment in order to pass on this information to their grandchildren, with the result that the coach is somewhat delayed in leaving for the course and, traffic being what it is, many members of the party have had a snootful before we even clear Ludgate Circus. Indeed, it has to be recorded that a number of cartoonists who have rushed for the back of the bus to make sure the corks are not too tight in the champagne bottles, since they are

(*l. to r.*) Gavin Lyall, Ann Leslie, Rowland Hill, Norman Thelwell, Alan Coren, William Hewison, Geoffrey Dickinson, Harry Secombe, William Davis, Lord Mancroft, Chic Jacob, Richard Gordon, R. G. G. Price, Bill Tidy, Fenton Bresler, Miles Kington.

very nice guys and think about little things like that, are too drunk to stand by the time the driver gets into third gear.

All in all, it is a fairly genteel journey, with very little of any consequence getting broken, the one exception being an articulated truck outside an establishment where the party stops to recycle the grape, whose driver catches sight of Welsh Harry and immediately takes off to inform his family, having in his excitement failed to link the two halves of his

jockey like the rest of us, but has also got his feet under the table at the Horserace Totalisator Board, where he is Chairman and consequently a good man to know at the beginning of the flatracing season when the odds are very long and no-one has any information, with the possible exception of Chairmen of Horserace Totalisator Boards, who may be in a position to stop you putting your shirt on something already overdue at the glue company.

"Good morning, Lord Mancroft," I say, "what is the word on Dinsdale Lad in the first race?"

At this, I see him go very pale and whip

writing business), and the two disappear together into the landscape, very fast. In fact, there is none of our party in sight at all, since the racecourse is putting on a free lunch which is far better odds than backing second favourites for a place, and they are all at the trough, except for one or two cartoonists parked in the umbrella stand. Since I have ever scorned the handout, I prefer to stroll down to the rails and pass a few leaves of negotiable tender into the capable hands of Morry Levy, who will look after them until Dinsdale Lad romps home with next month's rent.

This is not a bad investment, especially for Morry Levy, since at the time of going to press Dinsdale Lad is still romping.

I am just strolling back, when who should I see but Where's Bill Tidy, who is called this on account of the other cartoonists look upon him as some kind of leader and when the chips are down or their nose is running or they can't get the cork out tend to start shouting "Where's Bill Tidy?"

"Good afternoon, Where's Bill," I say, very civil, "what do you know?"

"I am off to invest a considerable sum on Big Jake in the 2.30", says Where's Bill, "to wit, thirty-eight-pounds-and-eight-pee."

"That is a large sum in these difficult days," I say, "not to mention a somewhat curious one. I do not follow."

"It is very simple," explains Where's Bill, "I am doing it on behalf of the syndicate."

At the word syndicate, a clearing rapidly opens around us, and a number of the turf fraternity begin putting the rubber bands back round their sandwiches and making for the exit, and I must say that it is crossing my mind to do likewise, especially as Where's Bill is sporting a pair of dark glasses and has never made any secret of his Neapolitan in-laws. However, he soon makes it clear that the syndicate concerned is actually a group of cartoonists, the rest of whom do not wish to leave the area in which the free crates have been deposited merely in order to place a wager, and indeed could not have done so before the starter's flag since they are some five hundred yards away, which is a considerable distance on all fours; as Dinsdale Lad will tell you when he gets here.

"Perhaps you would care to wager one-pound-ninety-two?" continues Where's Bill. "It would bring the bet up to a round forty, which at five-to-one cannot be bad".

I have to decline, being unable to explain that I am on Shantung Lady which is already past the post, since if I

pantechnicon together, and if any citizen wishes to take advantage of the fact, there is ten tons of something lying in a yard just this side of Saffron Walden. Soon after this, we arrive at Newmarket, and it is clear from the outset that this is a very toney meeting, the car park being stocked largely with Rolls Royces from which a number of tall citizens in sheepskin coats and corduroy hats are stepping and being somewhat miffed at the sight of a charabanc with cartoonists falling out of it and frightening the horses.

It is here that we meet up with Lord Mancroft, who is called this by everyone on account of the way he uses his fork and has suits almost as good as the bookies and is generally known on and off the course as a gentleman; what this guy's real name is I never hear, and anyway names make no difference to me, because the chances are that no matter what name a guy has, it is not his square name. The Lord has a number of things going for him, on account of he is not only a word-

the binoculars up to his face in the hope of being mistaken for someone entirely different.

"Please, Big Al," he says, "kindly remember the nature of the premises upon which you and I are chewing this particular slab of fat. We are not currently trading pleasantries in Small Nat's Elite Casino And Grill. Since I am endeavouring to put the Tote on easy street, an activity which is currently being quoted at around 7-4 against, I cannot afford to further alienate the bookmakers by handing out such privileged information. Bad enough they already think I am removing the bread from their mouths, without word getting out that I am setting up as Prince Monolulu. Citizens behaving in this wise have been known to wind up off Tower Bridge in a concrete homburg."

At this point, Eton Pete Dickinson moves up alongside on the strength of an Old Etonian tie which he says belonged to his grandfather (which only goes to show how tough things are getting in the

"Is there no alternative alternative society?"

do so everyone will wish to grab a piece of the action, thereby doing untold damage to the starting price. So I murmur something, and retire to the rails, to watch Shantung Lady come in at fourteen-to-one. Unfortunately, where she comes in with this nice price is number seven, and this is not a day on which the bookies are paying out seven places. Big Jake walks home by a length, and the cartoonists immediately celebrate by buying champagne for everybody. Well, not exactly buying, but at least they are prepared to let non-cartoonists near the crate for a brief period.

I am rapidly turning out to be the one bright spot in Morry Levy's day, and as any punter will tell you, as soon as a bookmaker starts stitching a welcoming smile on whenever you canter past his immediate vicinity, it is time to pack up and go into the shoe business. I do Tom Cribb in the Three O'Clock, which is the signal for Tom Cribb to do me by leading from the off and only losing his taste for the front in the last furlong. The

confetti is still falling around me when a very goodlooking doll who has been noting the proceedings murmurs "There's more fools know Tom Cribb than Tom Cribb knows," which shows she is not only good to look at but also has brains behind the mascara, which is not surprising on account of she is Katharine Whitehorn and a boon to any race meeting. I would have spirited her away to the tea-tent in the days when I had money, i.e. prior to two o'clock, but as it is I need the remaining collateral for the 3.30, in which an animal called Kiboletto is, I have it on very good information, as safe as the Bank of England.

Unfortunately, it is also as fast as the Bank of England.

It is as I am making my way back to the Members' Enclosure, a source of considerable grief to Morry Levy who is hoping, it being twenty minutes to the last race, for my co-operation in chipping in towards the swimming pool for the country estate I have already bought him, that I notice what appears to be a celebration in a glass box above my head. This box contains the *Punch* citizens, and in consequence I make my way there, hoping to put the arm on someone for a stake. It turns out that these citizens have been watching the entire proceedings on television, and not venturing down to the rails to listen to information, watch the odds, examine the horseflesh, and so forth, and in consequence have been doing such unprofessional things as betting on nags bearing the same name as their aunts etcetera. This, as any punter will tell you, is the worst possible way to lay scratch, and I do not have any explanation as to why these citizens are holding fistfuls of folding paper while I am in funds to the tune of 26p, unless it is that aunts do not have names like Dinsdale Lad, Kiboletto, Tom Cribb, and so forth, which is a good thing for amateur punters.

"Well, Big Al," says William the Editor, "it looks like things turned out pretty good, after all. All we need now is someone to write up these very enjoyable proceedings."

"Please do not look at me, William the Editor," I say, "on account of I am having the sort of day I wouldn't wish on a dog, even if it had just been beaten a short head with my mother's savings on it. There are many other hacks here who are able to write up the proceedings. I am sure you could persuade them to do same."

"I doubt it, Big Al," says William the Editor. "Nobody else needs the money."

He has a point, at that.

"He's asleep. Without the sound he'd fall over."

"David's off sick."

BERNARD HOLLOWOOD'S

Teleview

Martin Clinch's greatest ambition was to achieve notoriety as a television pundit. For twenty years he had campaigned as a do-gooder, espousing every liberal and democratic cause that hit the headlines and throwing his weight on the side of decency and commonsense in every political and social controversy.

His progress was meagre. He stood for Parliament as an independent and lost his desposit. He wrote a dozen books advocating policies already accepted as inevitable by progressive radicals of left and right and managed to get two of them published and remaindered. Newspaper editors considered him a reliable-enough contributor on stock topics and sometimes asked for his views when their papers needed "balance" to maintain non-party attitudes. Letters signed "Your obedient servant, Martin Clinch" appeared with predictable regularity in all the leading newspapers and magazines.

He was considered "safe" by steam radio and was often heard in *Any Questions?*, *Both Sides of the Fence*, *Topic of the Moment* and similar discussion programmes. Martin Clinch's *Letter from London* was broadcast weekly to Australia, Canada, Latin America and Fiji.

But in television he got nowhere. Every day brought topics on which he held sound views and good background knowledge, and every day, almost, he expected a summons to the TV Centre or Television House. It never came.

He had an excellent voice, photogenic features, his own hair and a good presence, and he had once been voted one of Britain's ten best-dressed men by the *Tailor and Cutter*. His failure to make the grade in TV baffled him.

In desperation he phoned Tarquin Totteridge, whose name had been household words for three decades and could still sell cans of catfood by the trillion when mentioned in a television commercial. Totteridge was flattered by Martin's approach; he had attended a very minor public school and in consequence looked with awe on the products of Winchester.

"Come down for the weekend, old boy," said Totteridge, "and bring your tennis racket. We don't dress, but there'll be church on Sunday morning."

Martin motored to Bournemouth on the Saturday and was closeted with Tarquin for five hours of instruction broken only by four sets of singles and two of doubles.

"The telly," said Tarquin, "isn't really interested in people with orthodox opinions. They are too thick on the ground. Practically everyone nowadays is humanist, democratic and progressive, so it's jolly difficult to get bitter controversy on the box. If you remember, I really got going during the Petkoff affair. All the do-gooders welcomed him to Britain for the Cold Peace talks: I took the opposite line and said we should try him for murder. As a result I was on the box nightly for nearly a month.

"And I kept it up by defending all manner of lost causes. But of course I had rivals, competitors who'd support the proposition that two and two make five if they thought it would attract the attention of television. When everyone was cheering the expansion of university education Monty Friend came out with the grim slogan, 'More BAs means more BFs' and you know what happened to *him*. Then when decent people everywhere became disgusted by the slaughter in Vietnam the young genius W. Aggner earned himself a regular spot in *Panorama* by praising America's inspired attack on the outposts of communism.

"And I don't have to remind you about Wolf Nocker, the MP who made it by urging the repatriation of tinted immigrants; about Barnie Grand, the impresario, who coined the expression 'Napalm does no harm'; Rolf Battersby, who claimed that battery farming yielded tastier food and rescued dumb animals from night starvation; Ennis Rickard, who defended religion when it was dying; Jim Pokerton, who attacked sex when it seemed set for popularity; and Mostyn Buck, who stated that women, Negroes and the poor were victimised by nothing but their genes. They are all telepundits now."

Martin Clinch thanked his mentor and promptly penned a letter to *The Times* in which he defended environmental pollution as a healthy reaction to "flabby sentimentalism". Two days later he got half an hour on *Late Night Line-Up*.

"Now I want you to face the camera and answer my questions about nudism, but for God's sake don't say anything controversial!"

HAPPY ANNIVERSARY, TED!

"We never put anyone behind bars, without good reason."

"Heathen bloody savages!"

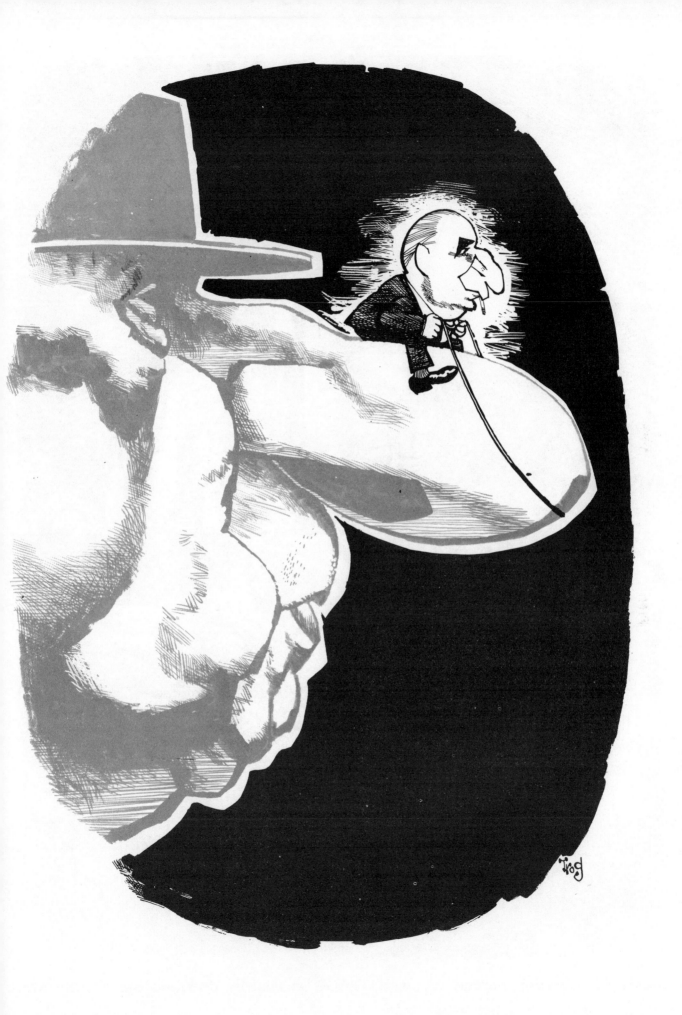

Due to circumstances beyond his control, TROG will not be drawing a cartoon this week

"It can't be for me—I'm the Sheriff."

"The arrangement's over, Cyril—you'll have to choose between us."

Who Needs An Embassy?

asks PETER PRESTON

A little while ago, much at random, I found myself in Rawalpindi: and there resolved to take tea with our chaps at the embassy. Pleasant, welcoming chaps, with a nice line in PG Tips; and a pleasant enough little office block of an embassy, pock-marked by the odd missile, defecated upon by the odd passing hound. My taxi went there swiftly, a matter of habit: but nix. Barred doors, broken windows, and the Gone Away sign. Kindly apply to HM Embassy, Islamabad.

Now Islamabad, a kind of cut-price Brasilia, is ten miles down the road, an enduring folly of Ayub Khan's quest for grandeur. We drove in search. We arrived and circled wanly for well over and hour, accosting passing peasants, policemen and civil servants. None had the vaguest notion where the embassy was. At last, and purely by chance, chugging down a track far beyond the American library, a building akin to a sawn-off Hilton emerged from the dust clouds. We toured round it, looking vainly for an entrance, then parked at the rear, near a gaggle of rickshaw wallahs and snoozing beggars. A guard stepped aside to reveal a line of gently stinking dustbins, a clutch of dismembered vehicles and a mesh of tunnels and staircases à la Clockwork Orange.

Ten minutes later I discovered the putative entrance. Twenty minutes later, after surveying HM Noticeboard ("Returning secretary must sell squash racket"), I found a mandarin, tea and digestive biscuit. Did he like it out here much? Well, it was very quiet. Did they get any excitement? Only when the Pak Army performed manoeuvres on the scrub wastes outside his window. Didn't it all seem rather, er, grandiose? Ah, well the dear old FO had planned it under the total misapprehension that Pakistan would still be a big and united country on completion. Meanwhile, another cup of tea . . .

Such a prolonged diplomatic ordeal is not, of course, unique. The search for a British Embassy—in Rabat, Rangoon or Reykjavik—is frequently extended and obscure. But never before, not even in the depths of the ambassadorial cocktail circuit, have I wondered so starkly what the point of it all was. Several hundred thousand pounds' worth of stainless steel, plastic sheets and Oxbridge graduates stuck anonymously in a shrinking military firing range. Did they ever see the President? I asked. Indeed, only a week or two before: he'd hired a train and carted the entire diplomatic colony five hundred miles south to harangue them on his country estate.

Memories of Sir Val Duncan came flooding back, the FO investigation long ago (say 1969) which attempted to answer one appalling question: what do diplomats actually do? And, stunned by that answer, reeled on to suggest spheres of influence henceforth and areas of maximum concentration (say Europe and America). Soft (lo), is that the music of a sphere of concentration wakes my costly doze?

Without doubt, and admittedly, matters do gradually improve. My Whitehall crusaders are very fond of their purposive statistics: like 809 executive grade counsellors now busily employed, against 515 in 1958, like 30,000 bits of export intelligence wired back to London every year as against 7,207 in 1958. But every so often the shimmery surface of Foreign Office cool lies shattered. It splintered, for me, in Islamabad. It cracked again a few weeks ago when the inevitable, inexorable Commons Expenditure Committee examined the business of Our Place in Rome.

The Rome Embassy, it may be recalled, rose amidst architectural groans and accountants' wails to completion in 1971 (at a solid million or more). It further presents a splendid open frontage on the otherwise cramped Porta Pia. Lovely, said some critics: horrendous, said the Expenditure MPs. We (that is, you, me and Sir Alec) own five acres in the Porta and the ambassador (that is Sir Patrick Hancock) has his Villa Wolkonsky, submerged in eleven acres of garden, woods and heart-lifting springs. Meanwhile, notwithstanding sixteen solid acres of eternal Crown land in the core of the city, we've been paying £107,000 a year for counsellors and secretaries to rent rooms and homes around Rome. The Committee, discovering this state of affairs drifting back a full 25 years, went smokily berserk.

Why does Peter Walker keep sending snotty notes to Harry Hyams when the FO have their own negative versions of Centre Point losing money throughout the world?

And the two strands of experience inevitably coalesce. In the last couple of decades we've built embassies in Kampala and Colombo, Saigon and Stockholm, Monrovia and Madrid, Ottawa, Oslo and a dozen more. Pretty sumptuous spots, by and large, as visitors to Bonn or Buenos Aires will testify. Villas in their natural gardens. Graceful abodes of the type the old picture section at Public Building and Works loved to furnish with a Henry Moore or Barbara Hepworth. But, simultaneously, the true tide has run the other way.

Duncan rippled its blue facade when he exalted commercial rather than political functioning. Yet the ancient, essential anchors have held firm. Whilst Duncan views the Service as, essentially, a squad of financial artisans, the Service still basks in the trappings of Empire. A counsellor may handle commerce, but the surroundings in which he handles it can be profligate with space, decorated by a Hockney, exuding cultural chic. The FO may be a new breed of business touters, but the business doesn't operate in a milieu most businessmen would remotely recognise. Further, the conversion to commercialism remains lip deep.

Take Rome for example. Not the million pounds or the redundant acres, but the very notion of a fat new headquarters at this particular time. We are on the brink of the Common Market; a month or two will see us in, and

"*Now on page 3, where the little red locomotive jumps its tracks and starts deliberately smashing down the row of old buildings—hadn't you better stress that for years the élite power structure of the city did nothing towards solving urban problems?*"

"Thank God this only happens once a year."

probably in for good. What repercussions flow? The unity of Europe, in every Eurocratic opinion, leads to power in Brussels and standardisation all round. Same weights, same measures, same medical qualifications (already), same transferable labour force, same laws, same multi-national companies, same interests, same (in the end) European Parliament: your land is my land. It will not, obviously, come overnight, or even in five years. But it will come within the handful of time it takes the Rome Embassy to weather a little. And what will be the point of Sir Basil Spence's million-pound spacefiller then?

Her Majesty's Government quite properly sees no point in favouring Scotland, Wales, Cornwall or the Isle of Dogs with a career diplomat, a vast staff and a lush outpost. While a spot of pageantry comes in useful about once a decade, the rest is a relaxed, natural infrastructure: the odd committee which the contacts industry itself creates because it needs it. Ten years hence can anyone in Whitehall imagine Sir Patrick Hancock's benighted successor nipping round to the Italian Foreign Office with Notes? There are telephones now; soon there will also be exceedingly centralised Brussels communication. Fred in one Commission office will merely have a word with Giovanni across the way.

One's back, in a trice, to that fundamental problem about what diplomats really do: and at once the clay-footed ghost of Sir Val begins to stalk consideration. Did the mandarins embrace his notions because they were right, or because they were the least they could hope to get away with? Putting aside pomp, circumstance and coffee with Sir Christopher Soames, was ever the increased commercial kick mere flummery? Our business attachés arrange British Weeks. I have been on British Weeks and I have seen the statistics a couple of years after revealing no permanent trading benefits whatsoever. (Great thighs on that imported blonde Beefeater, Carruthers.) More, I wonder painfully, how valuable were those thirty thousand bits of paper pouring back to London last year?

Once, in an airport transit lounge in Damascus, I discussed such questions with a young German salesman returning from the mystic East. I was sure our 23 senior men in Thailand did a grand job. He simply said, chillily, that Bonn had no formal relations with Peking, no embassy, no counsellors, no visiting trade missions, no Baden-Wurtemburg weeks in Canton. But they were still China's second biggest trading partner.

Put that experience in a Common Market context and delirium threatens. We shan't need Forfar fortnights in Frankfurt: they'll be an integral part of the package. We shan't need old

94

Etonian lingo-speaking fellows easing our nuts and bolts through the Itie Customs: there won't be any Customs. We shan't need wise birds in embassies sending brisk advisory notes to Birmingham: any business bent on survival will already have its own scouts patrolling the European "home market". A pack of superannuated company lawyers in Brussels, yes: the remainder, no. Just a few humble offices dotted around the Continent: the rest of the traditional parade simply swallowed by commonsense.

Obviously the diplomatic tribe en masse—squeezed between apathy about showing the flag in Angola and European absorption—won't take it well. Diplomats, like bottle washers and railway linetappers, have their safe little futures to fight for: plumb little permanencies worth an almighty struggle. When, in West Kensington, you hear about Hungarian envoys collecting 2,601 parking tickets in ten months; or import booze limits being set at 20 cases a year; or the UN growing stroppy because one minor trade official "smoked" eleven hundred cartons of duty-free cigarettes in fourteen days; or the plain fact that London's diplomatic population has swelled to top seven thousand—when you hear these charges you feel our men abroad must be much superior. Nobody stops for a second to consider, say, the British Embassy in Washington: 92 FO penguins, 110 military attachés, 180 civil servants, 300 chars, chefs and chauffeurs. We're not really different:

we're part and duty-free parcel of the true great international conspiracy.

So there is a fight and there will be continuing battle. Why else is Whitehall so obsessively sensitive about the cracks in the stilts at (where else) its new Madrid emporium, the Sir John Russell Pontinental? Why else are the dirtiest couple of words on the regular circuit Henry Kissinger (who shows that none of the trappings are necessary by flitting to and fro on passing Boeings)? Why else (after this) will my supply of free diplomatic dry martinis and cheese crackers be direly curtailed? The facts of technological life are making global diplomacy redundant; the facts of Europe make it a prime place to start trimming.

A suggestion: a property speculator friend has lately been jogging round our holdings in the Six—the glassy boredom of Bonn, the tasteful monolith of Paris, Rome and the rest. Assuming planning permission, how much might we raise by selling off? Maybe fifteen or twenty million in Rome, three or four in Germany, seven or eight in Paris. Lump in the fringe benefits, the odd mansions, the whole bargain basement (with inducements to our new partners to do likewise here) and the sums suggest a total round about our net contribution to the Community budget next year. Twelve months super free trial offer. It's enough to make Douglas Jay reach for the nearest Michelin.

"My wife doesn't like to crease the cushions."

And Who Needs Diplomats?

asks GRAHAM

"Good God, woman, we can't put on a banquet just because your brother and his wife are coming for the weekend!"

"I'll miss the old place."

"Did anything else come in the Diplomatic Bag apart from His Excellency's marmalade?"

"Remember the good old days when we used to have diplomatic incidents?"

Courtly Circulations

By WILLIAM HARDCASTLE

I'm prepared to bet that the other contributors to this issue of *Punch* have once again failed to strike at the bedrock of modern British journalism. Like the regular press critics, they will have forgotten to mention the Court Circular, or "Court and Social" as the *Daily Telegraph* more catholically describes its daily sweep over the courtly scene. But here I am to make good the omission, even if an intensive study of the subject has had a noticeable effect on my pulse rate and red corpuscle count.

The truth is that the sort of reportage that you get in the Court Circular does have a tendency to loosen the mind from its moorings and send it hunting for vague horizons. "The Queen", I read the other day, "attended Evensong and the laying up of the Garter Banner of the late Marquess of Salisbury (Chancellor of the Most Noble Order of the Garter) in St. George's Chapel, Windsor Castle."

My eye shifted a couple of inches down the page and there was "Queen Elizabeth, the Queen Mother, attended evensong and etc etc". Another inch further on, and off we went again: "The Princess Margaret, Countess of Snowdon, attended Evensong and etc etc". For a moment my practical journalistic approach to the subject remained in control. Why three separate paragraphs? Why not just say that all three attended evensong and etc etc, and save quite a lot of space? But then this mood of puzzlement and awe, coupled with the sensation of being lost in the Hyde Park underpass, took hold of me, and I had to turn to history to straighten up and fly right.

Apparently the scurrilous old *Times* started carrying a daily section of Court news back in 1785, but it was unauthorised stuff. The official Court Circular was the idea in 1803 of George the Third—he did have *some* good ones. It seems that he was fed up with the mis-statements that were being printed, presumably by *The Times*, about his goings-on.

On the other hand *The Times* itself decided to slap the Coat of Arms on the top of the daily column in 1901—thought it added tone, no doubt—and the *Daily Telegraph,* never one to let Printing House Square take a trick, quickly followed suit.

There was a time when *The Times* used to get its own copy of the Court Circular, inscribed on heavy vellum and dispatched across town from the Palace each nightfall. But today the process is less stately. The secretaries of the various Palaces—Buckingham, St. James's, Kensington, Clarence House, Windsor Castle, and so on—prepare their little pieces each afternoon. The Duke of Kent has done this, Prince William of Gloucester that, and Princess Margaret the other. With these

"If there's another water shortage we'll all starve."

reports in from the branch offices, the Master of the Household runs his eye over them, adds his own touches, and then rings up the Press Association.

And there it is—Boy Scout Rallies, diplomatic receptions, layings of foundation stones, and all —for the grubbiest copy boy to tear off the news agency ticker in any newspaper office. The Buckingham Palace PRO assured me, incidentally, that there is no copyright involved, which in these days of grasping agents is nice to know.

Granted it's not the most immediately compulsive form of journalism. "The Duke of Edinburgh, as President, this morning attended an Extraordinary General Meeting of the Central Council of Physical Recreation at Park Crescent, London. Lord Rupert Nevill was in attendance". There may be a story there somewhere, but it doesn't exactly leap out at you. But while mysteries remain—why an *extraordinary* general meeting?— why mention Lord Rupert Nevill?—what's the significance of Park Crescent?—there are other even more curious aspects of the newspaper pages on which these terse communiques appear.

If you inspect them carefully you will notice that after the messages from Windsor Castle, Buckingham Palace and points east and west, a thin black line is drawn. And that's where the money begins.

A lot of people may be fooled into thinking that the rest of the fine print on the Court Pages—the Forthcoming Marriages, the Receptions, the Luncheons, the Dinners—all come from the same unsullied source. No so. Most of this material—the bulk of the Court Page, in fact—is paid for at the rate of £2 a line. Which makes one wonder about the old principle of separating editorial material from advertising, but no matter.

The other day in the *Daily Telegraph (The Times* didn't get this one, which I calculate cost somebody a cool £18) I stumbled on an item that was both stupefying and fascinating at the same time:

"Mr. Edward du Cann MP was entertained to dinner last evening at the Cafe Royal by Colonel J. F. E. Pye. There were also present Major Generals V. H. J. Carpenter, H. C. Goodfellow and E. H. G. Lonsdale and Brigadiers T. A. K. Savage and R. A. J. Eggar."

Now there are two things you can do when you stub your toe on something like that. You might wonder what Mr. du Cann, a nifty City operator, is doing with all those military gentlemen. A military unit trust, perhaps? Or you can switch to the crossword. Indeed you can spend your life puzzling why "Two receptions for the Friends of Malta were held at the home of Mr. and Mrs. Basil

"He firmly believes laughter is the best medicine."

Lindsay-Finn, 64 Avenue Road, London, N.W.8, on Tuesday and Wednesday, April 18 and 19" (£14 there). Or you can turn to the simpler challenge of the chess problem.

Peregrine Worsthorne, now a loud editorial voice in the land, began his journalistic career as Court sub-editor on *The Times*. The main job was to get the titles and precedents right, but problems did arise from *The Times* rule of putting the Forthcoming Marriages in alphabetical order. There was always the fond father who wanted to see his debutante daughter's name at the top of the list and was ready to lay on a good lunch to achieve his objective.

In overall charge of these broad acres of our more serious daily press—though to be fair, the *Guardian* will have none of it—are the social editresses, Miss Margaret Alexander in the case of *The Times,* and Miss Mollie Taylor of the *Daily Telegraph* who has been at it, girl and lady, for nigh on fifty years. Indeed, she crossed over from the dying *Morning Post* in 1937.

Miss Taylor misses the days of the great country house occasions and the endless balls. She feels there is a strong commercial taint to many of the functions that are so enigmatically reported on her pages today. But she often gets more stuff than she can handle and items like, "Viscount Rothermere greatly regrets he was unable to attend the memorial service for Lord Rank yesterday," may get squeezed out, never to see the light of day.

The biggest trouble arises when there is an important State Visit and as many as ten coaches in the procession. The Court Circular, which is printed free, lists the passenger load in each of them, and there is accordingly much less space for the £2-a-line business.

These overcrowded conditions do not exclude the occasional oddity. In the midst of the Receptions and Dinners and Engagements in the *Daily Telegraph* the other day I read, "Today is the anniversary of the end of the San Francisco earthquake in 1806". A good deal more interesting than a lot of stuff around it, perhaps, but where is the social significance? Did somebody pay £4.50 to put it in? Another mystery in this most mysterious branch of journalism.

I am assured, incidentally, that if Mr. Fred Lurch and Miss Maisie Throb of Railway Cuttings, Catford, wish to record their engagement in *The Times* they are perfectly free to do so at the usual rates, but somehow it doesn't seem to happen very often. It is also clear that the Court Pages are read with meticulous interest by a large body of people. Mr. Harold Evans, a man of splendidly egalitarian sympathies, decided to drop the Court

Circular when he began to edit the *Sunday Times* but the consequent clamour soon forced him to change his mind.

Mr. Evans had probably forgotten the lesson that I learned on my very first journalistic assignment in North Shields in 1938. I was sent out to cover the funeral of a local hardware merchant. My instructions were to stand outside the cemetery gates and "Get plenty of names—and get them right". That's basic journalism, folks.

"*That crummy movie deserved no more than three or four Oscars at the most.*"

100

"I still say British roads were never made to carry this heavy continental traffic."

UNITED I STAND

Trendy JOHN WELLS forms his
own political party

Much low abuse, up and down the centuries, has been heaped on the Wolf in Sheep's Clothing. This has been due largely to the influence of the Bible and other works of political propaganda, but the fact remains that public sympathy is very heavily biased in favour of the Sheep. To have maintained for two thousand years that the knock-kneed, snaggle-toothed, dung-spattered, soft-eyed and vacantly squinting fleecy imbecile was, in its youth at least, the image of God, has inevitably tipped the scales against its natural enemy, the tawny aristocrat of the steppes.

Those who habitually employ the figure of speech tend to dwell mentally on the yellow fangs, the malevolent eye burning with murderous glee in the act of deception. What the propaganda has blinded them to is the social humiliation of the wolf: the abject self-contempt it must feel as it goes off hunting every morning, under the eyes of the leering she-wolves and their sniggering cubs, with the Persil-white fleece and the four Kiwi-black polished trotters jiggling up and down on its back, a bouncing powder-puff rendering ridiculous the noble sweep of its own bushy tail, and a vacuously grinning sheepface nodding about on its snout, obscuring its keen vision.

As with animal society, gentle reader hanging from a strap in the Underground or awaiting the dentist's whistling drill, so it is, if Konrad Lorenz, Desmond Morris and the theorists of the Third Reich are to be believed, with the human.

In advocating the immediate formation of the Capitalist Party of Great Britain and Northern Ireland I am asking for nothing less than the liberation from shame of countless thousands of men, women and children at

"Father's never ceased to be amazed at the phenomenon of electricity."

present living in a shadowy world of half-truth and subterfuge: men, women and children who in this allegedly tolerant age are forced to live a lie, acknowledging a belief they dare not name: men, women and children who dread to admit, even to themselves, that they are practising capitalists.

Like the wolf, the capitalist has suffered cruelly at the hands of the propagandists. Like the proud ancestor of the Securicor Guard Dog, capitalist man's best friend, the capitalist receives little public sympathy for his lacerated sensitivities, the inner agonies he must experience in adopting the disguises and camouflages forced on him by a hostile society.

It is hard to imagine the depths of misery and self-loathing that must be plumbed by the capitalist today, secretly dressing up in a cherished pair of striped trousers, patent-leather shoes and a much-loved silk hat in the privacy of his inner room, surreptitiously puffing at a forbidden twelve-inch cigar and listening to the Stock Market Closing Prices on a hidden radio set, always in fear and trembling that the doorbell will ring, obliging him to throw himself into a denim playsuit, spray the Havana-laden air with an aerosol freshener, and romp vivaciously down to greet his "straight" Maoist friends at the door of his Chelsea mansion.

To have to pretend, endlessly. To have to practise capitalism, either as a solitary or in groups, under the pretence of "working for the community". To have to pay lip-service to the hated creed of Socialism, or worse to have to call oneself a Conservative when the idea of conserving anything is repulsive to one's purest acquisitive instincts. To be obliged to use euphemisms like "redevelopment" or "building homes" when ancient capitalist forms like "demolition" and "an enormous profit", from which the orthodox capitalist gets a sexual pleasure amounting to religious ecstacy, are forbidden. To see, worst of all, capitalist achievements for which one has worked in secret for years, exploiting millions of workers, buying up whole housing committees, pass without a word of public recognition; and to watch, like excommunicated Christians forbidden the comfort of burial in consecrated ground, as massive capitalist disasters are erased for posterity by glib government publicists as if they have never happened and the names of the fallen capitalists suppressed.

To suffer all this, and yet to witness the nation's lesbians and homosexuals throwing off the frocks and trousers of oppression to rally to the banner of the GLF. To see liberated women toss aside the bust bodice of slavery. To see immigrants and racist bigots, members of the Royal Family and religious extremists, all achieving political recognition and public understanding. And yet to remain dumb, shunned and without a public voice.

It is ironic that such oppression should exist in a country that officially calls itself capitalist. Communist countries have no such inhibitions: there red banners hang across the street, proclaiming communist dogma for the edification of backsliders: there a man can look his fellow-man in the face, without hiding behind a capitalist silk scarf or bandying with pseudo-liberal jargon, and say "I am a Communist".

Is it too much to hope that with the formation of the new Capitalist Party, the equivalent might one day happen here? That a mill-owner, casting aside at last the cringing manners of the Liberal, might stand and face his workers and say, "I am a Capitalist. I vote Capitalist. I live in a huge house far larger than any of yours, and have a larger colour television set. If you go on asking for more money I shall be forced to sell my wife's second car, throw the lot of you out of work, and go and exploit your proletarian colleagues elsewhere"? That brand-named products might one day have Capitalist propaganda printed on the packet, explaining to the exploited housewife that by purchasing Scharnhorst's Family Size Deodorant Squirt she has contributed directly to fourteen-year-old Dieter Scharnhorst's new £5,000 hi-fi installation? That one day the Mall might be hung with azure banners saying "Victory to the Capitalist Party of Great Britain and Northern Ireland in its heroic struggle to knock down St. Paul's Cathedral and build a new multi-storey car-park"?

In the imagination I can see it now. Bald heads so long concealed under hippy-style funwigs glinting in the sun, cigars erect in the marching ranks, silk hats at the high port, and beneath a banner embroidered on a blue ground, "Guildford Capitalist Party Solidarity With US Imperialism and Boo Sucks To The Ghastly Little Men Who Clean The Sewers", Capitalist Matrons covered with medals won in the Class War, tongues stuck proudly out at the walking wounded of the same conflict who gloomily line the route, hoping to curry favour with the occasional austere "Hurrah".

I beg you. Do not delay. Help us to realise this vision now. Let the sheep's clothing be returned to its rightful owner, for let it not be said that the Capitalist Party is lacking in compassion. Bid those whose real achievement has transformed our way of life and the very face of our land in these last years step from the shadows, and enter, proud, into their heritage. Initial membership is limited to fifty-five million.

"The gang-bang's off—she has a headache!"

Hi! I'm Michael.
Fly me.
Fly Concorde,
the easy option.

NEW YORK
108 DECIBELS

ALPHA CENTAURI
4.3 LIGHT YEARS

WEST LONDON SCRAP
MERCHANTS
300 YARDS ON LEFT

TREASURY
£1,000,000 SUBSIDY
WHEN NECESSARY

HEATHROW

DEPARTURE LOUNGE
4 DAYS

ANGOLA
1 FLAG PER HOUR

IN-FLIGHT MOVIE
2¼ HOURS

Yes, I've got daily flights (well, annual promotional tours) at supersonic speeds (over bits of the ocean) to the sunshine states of the world (and who knows, one day they'll let us land).

I've got great connections in the USA (noise levels permitting, which they don't), Hawaii (once upon a time), Iran (if they take up their options) and South America (depending). And France, of course, where they are as much lumbered with Concorde as we are.

I've got great connections in Heathrow!

I can easily arrange a trip up and, pending further subsidy, down Runways 1, 2, 3 and 4. And, if the mood takes you, there's a bus to the departure lounge, the air terminal, and the motorway flyover.

I've got great connections in the sunshine aircraft industry, and I want to keep it that way.

So why don't you phone the British Aircraft Corporation and take up an option right now? Tell them Michael sent you. And listen to that hoarse chuckle as they replace the receiver!

Fly Michael. Fly Concorde.

Hints to Chinese Businessmen

from MILES KINGTON, in London

My readers in Peking will be interested to learn of an article in the *Daily Telegraph* (a capitalist paper with a difference: it makes a profit) on how British businessmen should behave in China. As you know, at least a thousand of them will be arriving for the British Trade Fair in March. The *Telegraph* warns them to be polite at table and not start drinking before their host, to avoid taking photographs of military objects, and to refrain from making passes at waitresses. They also warn that taxis are hard to find, that foreign restaurants are rare and that the Chinese consider anyone who raises his voice angrily has "lost face". Neither, says the *Telegraph,* should one opt out of official tours.

Before you smile and say that all this comes naturally to any civilised being, may I point out that each country has customs which seem strange to the outsider? It seems likely that many Chinese will also be coming to Britain to do business in the near future. You should know now that there are many traps into which you may fall if you are not forewarned.

For instance, it is almost impossible not to find foreign food in London. There are countless good Chinese, Italian and French restaurants here, and many more which feature a curious mixture of all the national styles, but no English restaurants. The English style of cooking is very good and is confined entirely to an endless stream of English cook-books. If you ask specifically to be taken to a good English restaurant, your request will be immediately granted with a visit to a good Italian, French or Chinese restaurant. Do not complain; it is not good manners.

Taxis are plentiful but almost impossible to stop, especially if there is someone already inside. In England the possession of one quarter of a taxi's space is thought sufficient to entitle you to all the seats. Climbing into an almost empty taxi is thought impolite.

Once the English have finished with the main meal, breakfast, the next great ritual is the midday drinking. Do not cause offence by trying to get yourself a drink. It is done in groups and the drinks are paid for communally, as in China, each person taking his turn. There is an elaborate procedure to choose the first buyer involving meaningless formal phrases derived from Ancient English:

"Let me do this one . . ."

"No, it is my shout . . ."

"What will you name as your poison?"

"It is time for the other half . . ."

Sometimes it becomes obvious that one of the number is not buying enough drinks, whereupon he becomes subject to heavy group criticism.

British hospitality is a well-established custom. Your business contacts will say to you almost immediately, "You must come out on the town with me," or "I'll show you some of the sights," or perhaps "Let me take you to the high spots in London." Do not show disappointment when this promised tour of the great attractions of London turns out to be a visit to a restaurant, a drinking place and a night club; it is thought very bad form to say in the middle of Trudie's Rendezvous that you would rather see the London Museum.

London buses are plentiful and cheap; they come in groups of five. When the conductor visits your seat, state your destination in a loud voice. He will then say: "You want a 27 going the other way, mate."

Do not enter into political discussions. As you know, the country is riven between the followers of arch-conservative Heath and the arch-conservative Wilson, but it is not considered that foreigners would understand the fine distinctions between them, and it would indeed take many years of study to appreciate the subtleties of the position. It is permitted to make general remarks such as, "Things could be worse," or "I remember when you could go on a day excursion to Shanghai and still have change from ten bob."

The favourite English drinks are French wine, keg bitter (a sweet brown mineral water) and whisky. The latter is made in the northern provinces of the country and served in very small glasses; it is customary to drink it quickly before it evaporates. From these provinces comes also a delicacy known as Scotch egg, which is never served till it is very aged.

English conversation is largely an exchange of pleasantries at which you are expected to smile heartily; businessmen especially are fond of long involved folk stories about travellers which involve them in untold indignities. It is thought very bad manners not to laugh at these disasters. Business communication is confined almost entirely to the telephone and letters, which are usually efficient in Britain, though this is never admitted. In fact, a diatribe against the telecommunication system is often a short cut to social popularity.

It would probably take a lifetime to master the intricacies of British social life and there are many Britons who never manage it. As Chinese, you should not even try; as long as you are prepared to express qualified enthusiasm for everything and to answer the question: "Which school did you go to?", you should be all right. The only really bad mistake you can make is to praise the way Britain is forging ahead in the modern world, as this kind of optimistic talk is considered quite unrealistic and dishonourable.

Finally, a word of warning about photography. You are quite safe as long as you keep to photographing the soldiers and military installations at Buckingham Palace, Horse Guards Parade, etc. But do not be caught taking pictures of ordinary things in the street—there is nothing that arouses more suspicion than a Chinese photographer paying attention to, say, a cat or a dog.

" You want Patel the Bank, Patel the Supermarket
or Patel the Plaid Cymru?"

RODERICK FLANN

Why Zsa Zsa Gabor cannot go on without tea

HOLLYWOOD, Saturday.

"DARLING," said Zsa Zsa Gabor, the hottest thing out of Hungary since Bull's Blood and Budapest Goulash, "have a cup of tea."

Tea! Good grief. There is nobody quite like Zsa Zsa. The last time I had talked to her, in Miami seven days ago, she had asked the waiter for a nice cup of tea and a silver bowl of water for Mister Genghis Khan, one of her three Shih-tsus.

Now it was time for me to light the blue touch-paper and sparkle with the incomparable Zsa Zsa once again. Over a cup of tea. Only this time, Zsa Zsa was mother. Fantastic. Nothing seems to dim her wattage. "You know me, darling," said Zsa Zsa, "I'm so headstrong. I love a cup of tea."

When she told me this, I said: "I must be the only person to have found this side to your character." Her eyes flashed golden, like two Balkan beacons, winking, as it were, the twin cities of Buda and Pest. She reminded me of the last time we had talked over tea. "It seems so long ago," I said. And she said: "Darling, that's what you think!"

She broke off. "With or without?" asked Zsa Zsa Gabor. I asked her to give me one lump. Which she did. "Fantastic," I said, but declined a piece of Battenburg. Dusk was falling over Bel Air. It was getting late. And dark. Time seems to flash past when you're talking, frankly, with the world's most glittering woman. I began to regret my dinner date with Sean Connery. Zsa Zsa wanted a piece of cake. So I handed her one.

Then because she was so clearly in a relaxed and intimate mood, I decided to take a gamble. I asked Zsa Zsa Gabor

about men. "Darling," she said, "men will be men." As though that explained everything, which of course it did. Had it always been like this? "I don't know what you're talking about. Men have always been part of my life. Sometimes they come, sometimes they go. You know me, darling."

Certainly, I did. Finishing off the last mouthful of tea, I put the cup back down on its saucer. It was time to leave Zsa Zsa living her hectic life for another long week . . .

WIT

HOW SPLENDID to be Sir Max Aitken! To have travelled the world, but still discover that there's nowhere quite like England. To live like a rajah in some Surrey hideaway, command the admiration of your peers, enjoy the devotion of many British readers and have the loot tucked away in the safest of all investments—British newspapers.

Now I discover (over lunch at his London club, not a stone's throw from the Palace of H.M. The Queen, and well within earshot of the clip-clopping of soldiers passing by on their fine horses on the march to their barracks) that Sir Max is no slouch when it comes to humorous anecdotes.

As the champagne worked its magic spell, he leaned across and told me: "Roddy, there was an Englishman, and Irishman and a Scotsman. And that's the way it ought to be!"

AGREEABLE

"WHERE have you *been*?" quipped Paul Getty, as I joined him and his guests for a picnic aboard his yacht in the South Seas, quite near to some of the loveliest Commonwealth islands, the other evening. "We've all been waiting!"

I must introduce Paul to Racquel Welch sometime, who once kept the Aga Khan waiting for almost a quarter of an hour, I

hear, when her plane was delayed on the way to join Jackie Onassis and Sean Connery for an evening's bridge.

As the sea bobbed laughingly at the side of Mr. Getty's yacht, mingling with the tinkle of a thousand glasses and necklaces, "It must be quite a relief to find that I've made it at last," I said. "After all, it can't be much fun to be the richest man in the world," I suggested, "surrounded by beautiful stars on a starlit night and have no one to write about it!"

"Not at all," said the extraordinary Mr. Getty, "as a matter of fact, I was thoroughly enjoying it . . ."

Lovely actress Pam Brunner's two-week marriage to Bolivian tin millionaire Serge Dreyfus is over, friends of the cordon-bleu heiress who once had a walk-on part in *Waggoner's Walk* are saying. "It was good while it lasted, we had a wonderful life together. But then I got bored," says Pam. "Maybe it's destiny."

SUNDAY EXPRESS

Reality

THE yen flutters. The deutschmark marks time. The lira is in full retreat. The dollar takes refuge in splendid isolation.

Once again, the pound stands alone, swimming against the tide. As it did at Trafalgar. At Sebastapol. At Mafeking. At Ypres. And Dunkirk.

Let us not be surprised that our former enemies show us no gratitude. Or that our one-time ally reverts to its ancient policy of all aid short of help. We are ready for the next Battle of Britain.

Let us rejoice in the opportunity to show our faith in the ultimate victory of our Anglo-Saxon currency, pinned to our masthead over the tea coupons carried by lesser breeds.

Devalued and decimalised, taxed and surtaxed, it remains still our pound. So altogether, let us chorus our financial anthem—Salute to Sterling!

Touching

WILLIAM RICHMAL CROMPTON is the boy nobody noticed. "Spotty" or "Stinker" or "Pig-face" was what his pals called him when they bothered to call him anything. He might have passed through life a useful anonymous half-wit. But last week, he hit the headlines.

His hamster, Ian Smith, died from over-exposure due to a failure in the dorm's central heating. All right, it was oil. But it could so easily, so nearly, have been gas.

So he flushed its lifeless body down the plug-hole, no doubt murmuring an eloquent though silent prayer to that God who watches over hairy little creatures. But he did not stop there.

Using all the resources of the school's stinks lab, he manufactured a bomb. And he knew

"Compliments from below stairs and many happy returns."

where to put it. Under the headquarters of the Transport and General Workers Union.

Some may blame him. Others may think his eccentric behaviour the result of watching too much violence on TV.

We do not. We say—bravo William Richmal Crompton! You acted for Britain. You are part of our history.

Dreams

DID you read that Harold Wilson had the cheek to accuse Edward Heath of living a fantasy life?

Our Prime Minister is the most colourful politician of this century. Beside him, Bonar Law was a nonentity.

He is a greater sailor than Jonah. A greater organist than Dr. Schweitzer. A greater economist than John Bloom. A greater orator than Sir Max Aitken.

Is there a more eligible bachelor in Christendom, except perhaps for Prince Charles and the Pope?

Some fantasy! Some cheek!

Put that in your pipe dream and smoke it, Mr. Wilson.

HOW LONG MUST OUR CHILDREN WALK IN FEAR?

By A. J. P. MAUDE

BEFORE very long the Government is going to have t make up its mind what to do about education. Do we nee more or fewer schools? Do we, in fact, need schools at all

There is not much doubt what answer the silent majorit would give to this question. They would say that educatio is an expensive luxury. And they would be right.

The lefties and the trendies, of course, would disagree—and with good reason. They know the fantastic price we have to pay for schools—more, in any one year, than the cost of Concorde.

The Marxists and Maoists who have infiltrated our society argue that we cannot afford both. They are right—but for the

wrong reasons. They want to se Concorde dropped in favour c more schools.

Thus, for the sake of the crackpot theories, they would se back supersonic travel by tw thousand years. They woul hand trade supremacy to th Americans and the Japs. Mear ile, a new generation made erate out of taxpayers' money uld be lapping up the ngerous pap of the drop-outs d the drug-takers. Britain uld be finished.

Consider the havoc that educan has wreaked already. The trial was the direct consequence of children being able to ad. The Poulson case shows at a little learning—especially arithmetic—is a dangerous ing. The Americans' humiliatg withdrawal from Vietnam as the result of signatories ing able to write their own mes. And would we have filth television if all those freakish ript-writers had never learned type?

Look at campus riots. Look at the antics of so-called students. Look at the farcical experiment of comprehensive schooling. When will we realise that there would be no drug-taking in schools if there were no schools?

Until the middle of the nineteenth century the mass of people in this country were illiterate. Yet Britain flourished. We built factories as fast as the bricks came out of the kilns. Our ships ruled the oceans. Our Empire—created largely by men who could not even read a map—was at its zenith.

All that has gone—and for what? So that a few long-haired novelists may have their puerile outpourings immortalised between the covers of a Penguin book.

Schools are a passing fad, imposed on us by well-meaning do-gooders who thought they had found a way of keeping ragged children out of the chimneys and the mines. But we have central heating now, and coal is becoming rapidly a thing of the past.

Close down the ramshackle Department of Education and divert the vast sums spent on schooling to the development of a swing-wing supersonic airplane. The country will be happier for it.

CURRENT EVENTS
John Gawdon

IN late February Mr. You-know-who asked us to believe in his cocky way that Mr. Heath was behaving like Muhammad Ali.

I am told that the Ali-Bugner fight had already taken place before these ill-judged words were uttered. So perhaps Mr. Wilson is not wholly to blame for Joe Bugner's defeat.

But isn't it extraordinary that the man who claims to lead the Labour Party should publicly compare a British Prime Minister with an American boxer?

What does Mr. Wilson say about this charge? Not a word.

THE cheeky Belgians refuse to buy Concorde. Very well. That is their own affair. But isn't it remarkable that we still maintain an expensive embassy on Belgian soil? And that British bigwigs wine and dine in Brussels restaurants?

Not a penny of our hard-earned cash should go to these upstart foreigners until they come to their senses.

A Pitlochry heating consultant with no previous convictions is dragged out of bed

by the police at three in the morning. At public expense, he is brought to London and charged with stealing four lemons valued at 65p.

I say nothing about this case, which is still sub judice. But isn't 65p for four lemons a bit steep, even in these inflationary days? If I were the Minister responsible, I hope I would have the humility to resign.

WASN'T it good fortune for Sir Gerald Nabarro that he wasn't in the news last week? Otherwise I might have had something to say about it. As it is, my lips are sealed. He is a lucky man.

IN describing those Fife magistrates as two-faced hypocritical prigs last week, I am told that I may have given the impression that they were two-faced hypocritical prigs.

I was relying on a transcript clipped by my reporter from a local newspaper. I now learn that his facts were wrong. I am glad to set the record straight.

BUT how much better it would be if my reporter did his work properly.

Politics and Personalities   by CROSS-BENCHER

The Name of the Game

WHO this fine Sabbath morning feathers his arrow, stretches his long w, fills his quiver, poisons his rts, on the vasty fields of outh? Why, Jeffrey Howard rcher, the theatre-loving, newsaper-freelancing darling of the outh Working Men's Club, ho once ran ("very slowly") for reat Britain, and now climbs ry fast in the Tory party, and perates at the speed of light as ublic relations marksman for rrow Enterprises Promotions.

ike the clappers

★ Or, on the other typewriter, it could be Peter Kingsley rcher, barrister MP for a abour constituency which ounds like a firm of solicitors Rowley Regis and Tipton), in he bosky verdage of Chorleyood as he keeps body and soul part by combining hobby and rofession ("talking").

★ And how this miserable wintry Sunday eve fares the Disraeli of Beaconsfield as the ocsin sounds from the leafy

villages of South Bucks? Does it ring his withers at his mansion of Witheridge and reverberate around his greying nut at Knotty Green? Ask not for whom it tolls, it tolls for thee, Ronald McMillan Bell, Queen's Counsel who think women unfit to rule, amateur athlete who no longer dare run your nightly round for fear of liberated females prowling the byways, panting to unhook your clapper.

Pure research

★ Wherefore and for why, whither and moreover, yea and verily, columns like this will track you all down through the pages of Who's Who, punishing you through puns, beating you with your Clubs, torturing you with your Third Degrees, hobbling you with your hobbies, savaging you with cuttings, remaindering your Publications, numbering your divorces.

Just a trim

★ One-fingered time is yet hopping its grisly dance on the keys to spell out more such para-

graphs. The dilemma of Anthony Perrinott Lysberg Barber, who has never forgotten the short-back-and-sides of his Russian POW imprisonment, and now sits in the PM's ante-chamber—three chairs, no waiting. The bashing of Edward Stanley Bishop—which hand would he hold a crook in? The polling of Albert Edward Booth. The topping of Arthur George Bottomley. The passing of Philip Antony Fyson Buck.

Steady the Buffs

★ The beasts of Frederick Frank Arthur Burden, Chmn of the Parliamentary Animal Welfare Group. What Mrs. Joyce Shore Butler saw. Christopher John Chataway went thattaway. George Darling is no longer darling George. What leaks are seeping from Hugh John Dykes, recreation swimming? Our Nor-

thern edition will not print Miss Janet Evelyn Fookes.

Hire Purchase

★ Michael Foot is now on the other boot. The Opposition has shot the Government's John Marcus Fox. If wet, in Miss Joan Valerie Hall. Give me a Harold Lever and I will move the News of the World. Ernie David Drummond Money is in nobody's pocket.

They're open!

★ The Peter McLay Mills and the William Stratton Mills grind slowly but they grind exceeding William Watson Small. Pick up the David Weitzman's burden. Weave the warp, and warp the Robert Edward Woof.

★ It matters not whether your MP is known to the multitude, here all names makes news so long as I can find them in Who's Who.

Our Man in Kampala

Bit of a rush wid de copy dis week, world, dis Foreign Correspondent game got more in it than meet de eye, turned out wife number four knocked off de cleft stick on account of it a top-hole day for drying vests, wid de result that my hot line to de outside world bin holdin' up de clothes-rope out back till jus' now. Won't happen again, though: she gonna get three years for interferin' wid de freedom of de Press, soon as de Supreme Court soberin' up.

Still, it a dam' sight better filin' your own stuff, as I explained in my last article (wot just' bin awarded de famous Gobel Prize for Literature, de top Uganda gong for genius, £25,000 in used notes given by de gumment whenever it knocked out by a first-class piece o' spellin'), an' I damn glad most of de other correspondents currently gittin' de order of de boot.

In fact, dis week's hot story concernin' a sim'lar piece of legislation, only dis time in de ole dipperlomatic field. You no doubt bin hearin' elsewhere about how I givin' de well-known heave-ho to de British High Commission. From now on, ain't gonna be none of dis formal contact between de Uganda Gumment an' Acting High Commissioner Harry Brind, who damn lucky he ain't gittin' a poke in de conk, struttin' around in de pinstripe material and de polished boots an' claimin' he de direck link wid de Queen. I ain't got nothin' against de Queen, God bless her an' all wot sail in her, only she and Brind got to know their place; they occasionally forgettin' that I got a direck link, too, an' mine is wid de Almighty, and

he gettin' pretty choked off lately wid de way dis Brind item bin shovin' his nose into de pussonal affairs of His Emmisary On Earth, Special Agent Idi Amin, D.Litt., 007, winner of de Gobel Prize two weeks runnin' if I'm any judge.

Dis Harry Brind ain't gonna do any representin' no more. In addition to bein' de Foreign Press Corps, I now also de new Acting Acting British High Commissioner, wid special responsibility for dealin' wid de slow takeover of British property in Uganda, i.e. sendin' de Flyin' Squad round to change de locks an' hand out de one-way tickets for de next Dakota. De milliner jus' bin round wid de new hat, it got plumes comin' down over de ear, and I got dis spiffin' new dress uniform, it got Ammiral of de Fleet trousers, Air Chief Marshal jacket, an' de genuine ermine D.Phil.(Oxon.) gown fastenin' at de neck wid de VC, Iron Cross, an' Gobel Prize Medal and Bar. Dat what a High Commissioner ought to look like, a bloke wot stand out at de garden party, keep de waiters on de hop wid de old cucummer sandwiches, and not gittin' mistaken for a patron of de Montagu Burton Hire Purchase Department. Also got a big ceremonial sword, comin' in damn useful if anyone else's Ambassadors gittin' funny ideas.

Still, de main question remainin' unanswered: which are, do I get addressed as His Excellency President General Idi Amin, Esq., or President His Excellency General Idi Amin Esq., or General His Excellency . . .

Anyone got any ideas, I'll be down de used car lot.

A Nation of Greenfingers

With food prices escalating daily, the Government's Phase Four will now consist of a compulsory grow-it-yourself policy. MAHOOD reports from the top of the compost heap

"I've turned the front and back lawns over to wheat and if there's a glut the Russians will always take it off my hands."

*"What Henry doesn't understand is that when it comes to water-cress one **doesn't** think big!"*

111

DAD

a helluva swell guy

MOM

a living saint

SISTER

one sweet kid

A VISIT TO GRANDPA & GRANDMA'S

JUNIOR

a regular little man

THE MULTI-DIVORCED FAMILY'S WEEKEND VISITATION RITES

THE FAMILY, HAVING 'BROKEN DOWN' IN THE 1960'S, RETURNS TO MAKE IT UP IN THE 1970'S

FAMILIES ARE LOVE

PASSING THROUGH

EARTHA KITT talks to David Taylor

In this series of brief encounters, DAVID TAYLOR sets off each week, in the company of FFOLKES with his sketch-pad, for a drink and a chat with some of the celebrated· or distinguished people who are Passing Through London. Sometimes they get along famously, other times not . . .

I wasn't much taken by Eartha Kitt and I'd say for certain that she can't stand me. Nor can I do with prissy chihuahuas, two of which she was feeding with love, affection and giblets as we stepped past the outsize teddy into her dressing room under the Criterion. At this point, mind, I had no feelings either way. One of these Mexican midgets is called Tweety. He's very virile, she says, and comes from Torquay. "You look unhappy," I remarked idly, not to Tweety but to Miss Kitt, because she did. Miserable. That did it. "I am not unhappy. I am tired. There's a difference." And chuntering that the vibrations weren't right, she and Tweety stalked off down to the other end of the dressing room and assumed an histrionic air of frostiness. I said cautiously that I hoped she was enjoying this fresh stint in London theatre. "I don't usually do things that I don't want to." Full-stop. Tension. The telephone rang. Eartha Kitt, inexplicably livid at the suggestion she might not have been exciting, sensuous, wonderful and alive (her own summary, later, of her regular condition), snatched at the receiver and dropped it. It sank gurgling into Tweety's little water bowl. End of tension and, near as dammit, end of interview.

I have to hand it to ffolkes's diplomacy at this point for downing pencils, poker-faced, and interrupting events with a few well-chosen reminders of Miss Kitt's unique status as a face, an artiste and original star. "As far as I am concerned," she declared with real conviction, "I'm just a very natural, simple person. But I

114

"No willpower, that's his trouble."

recognise myself as being probably one of the only original individuals in the world—you don't want to be simply run of the mill." And seizing Tweety to her cleavage, she acknowledged that "Perhaps I am moody. It is because I don't like being surrounded by stupidity." Guess who. "I can only grow on things which I feel are enhancing me." I was clearly not such a thing. Despite her repeated conviction to the contrary, I had not arrived to chat to her predisposed to deny her treasured vibrations, in a mood to dislike. She'd convinced me all by herself.

This embarrassing edge on conversation was to last throughout the whole of our talk. She did finally mellow, dismissing me as "a poor baby", but not before we'd had it spelled out that on no account was a person so sensitive as herself to be approached with the suggestion she was sad. "It shows that you haven't even tried to understand. You have no idea what my schedule has been . . . the reason that the world is falling apart is because people are not caring enough about adding anything to it." Quite so. Beg pardon.

"It is, though," Eartha Kitt maintains, "just a matter of getting acquainted. It is the same with any audience." There are occasions there, also, when the magic fails to click. Monaco, for instance, where despite reports of a howling success in concert Eartha has vowed never to return. "No amount of money in the world can make me go back to a place I wasn't happy in . . . Only if you feel wanted is everything all right in the world." These two topics seem to preoccupy Eartha Kitt. Money she is scornful of.

"My tastes are very simple. All I ever wanted was three square meals a day. I think that I have coped with success. I have my sanity, I'm not a hard drinker, I'm not a dope addict. Like I sing in the song—*I am not sophisticated, I'm the sweet and simple kind.*" Was she looking, then, for that *old-fashioned millionaire*? "No. It doesn't mean that I want him when I walk off stage. Eartha Kitt sings that she wants him, she desires him, but not Eartha . . . It is the same with any woman in life. Or a little girl. You know, I cannot remember when anybody ever gave me a doll. For my little girl, I have collected dolls from all over the world, ninety countries; she has now one of the world's greatest collections of dolls." I was keeping my mouth tight shut. We left the subject of being wanted with Eartha's revelation that "All my desires come from my belly-button, not from the diamonds on my hand."

Self-respect, acclaim, are things which have to be earned in Eartha Kitt's book. She has earned it through sheer individuality, she maintains. "I have always been different. I think of myself as an artist rather than an entertainer. Very few people are artists." Part Cherokee, part black, part white, "I stood out in the crowd even when I was just picking cotton. I was a star. The best cotton-picker they had . . . Charisma, that's a word I like very much. It is something to treasure. I want there never to be a moment in my life when I feel that I am not exciting, sensuous, wonderful and alive." And that, tough luck on us, was where we came in.

PASSING THROUGH

ROBERT GRAVES talks to David Taylor

Everybody says how well I look," acknowledged Robert Graves, who did, "but in truth I'm feeling lousy." And with a cryptic disdain, "I am being slowly poisoned," he declared. Well, like most of the things he was to tell on this drowsy, sudorific afternoon, it was a long, entertaining and implausible account (this concerning an anti-depressant medicine which he claimed had been consistently misprescribed) which was dangled before us for its cogent, dramatic effect and then snatched away the minute that any pedestrian facts or hint of corroboration seemed set to interrupt the flow. Septuagenarian lovelorn poet, distinguished fusilier, the officially adopted son of a once-remote Majorcan village and the self-styled eccentric custodian of all things British to the core, he was choosing to indulge himself. Bizarre, fragmented anecdotes, sudden disconnected fancies, astonishingly detailed slanders, even a threat casually to extemporize some esoteric Hungarian folksong that sprang to mind, all combined to rout any conversational discipline. And what was left he contrived to punctuate by staring out of the window and remarking on the girls (who walk better now than they did), losing the thread, forgetting the names, pausing to cough, pausing. Yet despite these minor upsets, feeling peaky or not, Robert Graves sat and led us through his own special wordy fandango, making it clear it was a privilege, and making it very hard work indeed.

Graves had come to London for the play adapted from *I, Claudius* (who was 54 when he started to emperise, by the way) and was happy with the upshot despite a lukewarm press. He never travelled anywhere without a purpose, so he said, but he hoped to visit China. So was there a purpose in that? Only perhaps. "I went to Mexico for the Olympics," he announced familiarly, and told us his favourite story of how he's twice won a medal for poetry and views it as a feather in his cap. (His cap, which is black and floppy, incidentally, is something he wears all the time. Various local Majorcans have taken to doing the same since the recent issue of *Goodbye To All That* in translation on the island. Very rum.) Anyhow, "the first time it was a bronze medal, which I gave to a girl on Headington Hill who said that she collected junk. I haven't seen it since." Then the Mexicans awarded him a gold one out of gallantry after he gallantly arranged a convention there of poets, amongst them a Puerto Rican and a local homosexual who was quite a decent poet despite this dreadful handicap. We didn't get further details because he was suddenly reminded that our own Queen is descended from the Prophet and he once told her so. Graves has a similar lineage and, more than likely, so did we. Funny thing, the Moslem Code.

For most of his time, Graves is settled in the Majorcan sun, at Dejá, which is not what it was. For a start, it once had half a dozen carpenters and simple, peasant folk who survived by building walls. None of that now. Everybody's gone, gone to Palma chasing tourists, leaving the Graves feeling very neglected, bereft of servants and local colour, digging their own potatoes and making damson jam from the damson tree. Worse, "the track which used to go past the gate is now a metalled highway with motor-bikes and cars going round and round, hooting dismally." But the house is grand and spacious, is worth ten times what it was, and backs on to mountainous woodland which they frequently go and potter in. They have lived there for forty years, having fled England to escape Development. All of which is tiresome to Graves and led him off again.

Hopping swiftly through some half-forgotten tale about uranium near Dolgellau, mining copper in New Guinea, and the occasion he snubbed Mr. Edward Heath in the vestry of Southwark Cathedral, Graves picked on Hardy as one of the few poets he had ever met from a lengthy string of acquaintances that began, he claims, with Swinburne. He particularly liked Hardy and had stayed with him in Dorset. Graves and Mrs. Graves were

the first to use the newly-fitted bath. Of modern poets he is scornful. "It is free, but not verse. I have only met one new poet in the course of the last ten years and he was a very unhappy man. He was only able to produce during a really gloomy period during which his wife was prone to a series of miscarriages. When they stopped, so did he. Odd, isn't it?"

And so it went on. We covered ballet, which is in sad decline; touched on gardeners, who are not to be had for love or money these days; talked of his uncle Charles who worked for *Punch* and remarked on the way that Americans drop in uninvited; and listened to his tales from a visit to Hungary, where a friend has turned up an opera by Mozart, lying in a kitchen, and is sticking it together for posterity. Which is something that doesn't tax Graves, any more than did the fact that we'd been rummaging along for over an hour. "Don't say anything too disastrously true about me," he concluded, and as if this might be a liberty added on, "I think there is a degree in permissiveness which has been reached now which I find shocking. It destroys the old thing called love." And with it romance? "Yes, and with it poetry."

"There's a man outside says he's got some great pictures of Prince Philip."

DIVORCE
British Style

by MAHOOD

"It's Cynthia, she wants to know if we'd
like to come round and see the slides of
her divorce evidence against Rodney?"

"Try and push the divorce through during
the Freeze. I don't want to be landed
with an inflationary settlement."

"Mrs. Mayberry says she is sorry to bother you,
but could you come over and witness some
mental cruelty?"

"A right bloody Solomon *that* judge turned
out to be!"

"Could I have an adjournment, M'Lud? I think a last minute reconciliation is taking place!"

"How can I live with a man who boycotts South African fruit, Rhodesian tobacco, Greek holidays and Portuguese wine, but **not** Spanish au pair girls?"

"When the decree becomes absolute, it just means that Daddy will be replaced by a new model."

"Call that British justice—giving **me** custody of the kids?"

Queue Here for Asians

While it's true that most people who've offered homes to Ugandan Asians have done so out of the goodness of their hearts, it's also true that a few baser motives have been about. As in these typical letters intercepted on their way to the Resettlement Board.

"We're not anti-Common Market—we're just anti-onion."

Dear Sir:

You do not seem to understand the seriousness of my complaint of the 7th inst. I ordered my Asians at least three weeks ago, and there is still no sign of delivery. When we ordered a wart-hog from Harrod's for my young daughter Lavinia's 21st, it was there in five days.

Your poor service has already caused me considerable embarrassment: as a man of comfortable means, enjoying a respected position within the community and, I might add, a close acquaintance with several members of the Cabinet, I was ready, nay, eager, to offer the lodge cottage of my weekend residence at Angmering to a suitable Asian family. I required no remuneration from this, as you will no doubt have seen from my interviews in the Press and on TV, merely the satisfaction of knowing I had done my duty and of knowing that the British public would be able to see that no act of common humanity was too small for the chairman of Podsnutt Plastics Ltd., manufacturers of fine kitchen furniture since 1962.

The embarrassment has not been mine alone: my lady wife has already had to cancel a fully-catered Meet Our Asians garden party, at which we had every expectation of seeing no less a personality than Mr Michael Parkinson, the friend of a friend. As a result of this cancellation, considerable damage has been caused to my deep friendship with the Editor of our local paper, Mr E. G. Whitpoole, MBE.

May I expect delivery by the end of the month? If the items have not arrived by then, I'm afraid I shall be forced to cancel my order.

Yours faithfully,

R. J. Podsnutt

Dear Sir:

I understand you still got a few Asians available. What I'm after is a farely scruffy one, prefbly without shoes, and if there's one with a boan stuck through his conk, so much the better.

I wun't want him for too long, say about a fortnight, on account of Mr James Bleeding Anstruther will have had enough by then and agree to (a) mending the fence where his bloody kid rode his bike through (b) shut up claiming our lime tree is droping gum on his Cortina, why doesn't he put it in the garage where it belongs, we've all seen it by now, mate, and I wun't care, it's not even new, two previous owners (c) turn his hi-fi down, we're not all Andy Williams fans, or, alternately, buy sunnink else besides Moon Bloody River and (d) keep his dog off our cat Dennis.

Let's see how he likes having a nig-nog next door!

Yours truely,

Morris Foskett (Mr.)

Dear Sir:

I believe you have some needy Asians you wish to accommodate, and I should be only too glad to help out. I think they will find 17, Esterhazy Villas, very much to their liking, as there are already forty-three of their compatriots living there, in our spare room.

Of course, accommodation is fairly tight, but just last night, after my husband came back from taking our Alsatians for a walk, he said he'd noticed there was still a space under the sink upstairs. I know it isn't much, but in these difficult times, it's up to

120

each of us to help one another, I always say.

It's £12 per week per couple for the space, and £5 per child for the sink, no cooking, no pets, candle provided at cost. I look forward to an early reply.

Yours faithfully,
Anona Corkmantle

From Robin Wilcoxpott,
Current Affairs,
Midlands TV

Dear Sir:

As the chairman of TV's most successful Current Affairs programme, I find myself in the happy position of being able to offer free accommodation, including evening meal and continental breakfast, for the night of November 9, for up to 3 doz. assorted Ugandan Asians.

The sort of thing we're looking for is a bit vague at the moment, but we'll almost certainly need some who've been knocked about a bit (the *ideal* would be a bloke or, better, woman, who'd maybe lost a leg on the way to Kampala Airport, or got raped, something of that order), some who've lost everything they've owned, some who've left dependants behind, you know the sort of thing, I'm sure; you must have seen my programmes, everyone has.

One important thing: I don't want too many smiley ones, we're not after cheery buggers saying That's what life is all about, we'll just have to start again, it's great to be in England, any of that old tat. Pick out the right miseries, I'm certain I can leave it to you, and if they'd had a bit of Paki-bashing outside Stradishall or anything, so much the better.

Just one other teeny request: are you absolutely sure none of these characters is carrying anything contagious? I mean, God knows what they pick up in bloody Africa, beri-beri, smallpox, swamp fever, all that rubbish, and you know how warm it gets in a studio, bloody germs thrive on it like mad. Anyway, I know I can rely on you,

Yours in gratitude,
Robin Wilcoxpott

"*No, **you** tell him we've lost the Empire.*"

121

HEATH
on the latest
status symbol

"If you could find us something near Eton so that we can visit our son."

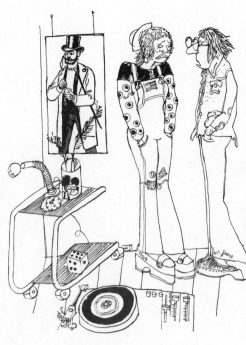

"*Before I let you in, you must promise that as a nuclear scientist you won't be making bombs in your room.*"

"*Look, Julia, I'm just as sorry as you are that an Asian family didn't move in next door.*"

"*Nigel and I would have an Asian family like a shot, but the cleaning lady said she'd walk out.*"

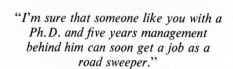

"*But Mother, they won't be here long, think of him as Peter Sellers!*"

"*I'm sure that someone like you with a Ph.D. and five years management behind him can soon get a job as a road sweeper.*"

"What do you mean by 'innocent'? Are you innocent as charged, innocent with extenuating circumstances, or innocent with a plea for clemency? Are you innocent of anything you are not charged with? We demand precision here."

A lot of trouble could be avoided if passports and visas really said what they meant. What we need are some new designs . . .

PASSPORTS FOR ASIANS IN AFRICA

Her Britannic Majesty's
Principal Secretary of State
for Foreign Affairs
Requests and requires in the name
of Her Majesty
all those whom it may concern
to allow the bearer to stay
put in Africa and not, please not,
throw him out, as if things weren't
crowded enough at Heathrow already
without having thousands of Indians to
accommodate, to which we append the
reminder that aid can be withdrawn
at a moment's notice as may
be necessary.

COUNTRIES FOR WHICH THIS PASSPORT IS VALID
PAYS POUR LESQUELS CE PASSEPORT EST VALABLE

VALID FOR ALL PARTS OF AFRICA AND FOR ALL FOREIGN AIRPORT LOUNGES

The validity of this passport expires:
Ce passeport expire:

At a moment's notice
....
unless reneged

NEW BRITISH PASSPORT FOR COMMON MARKET

The Passport Office, British Subjects Division, Brussels, Belgium, Requests all those whom it may concern to stamp this passport in the right place, check the photo against the bearer's face and let the bearer pass freely, as long as he conforms with the seventeen volumes of Community regulations, behaves obsequiously and doesn't try any of the old nonsense about being under the protection of, what was the phrase? — Her Britannic Majesty's this, that and the other; in the eventuality of his doing so, he should be reminded that the Queen herself has got to have a passport with this wording as well, so who does he think he is?

VISA FOR SCOTTISH FOOTBALL FANS

BRITISH VISA

Her Majesty's Government calls upon the citizen of whatsoever country in which the bearer finds himself, to turn the bearer over on his back, loosen his collar and remove the bottle from his pocket.

Note to bearer: This visa does not entitle you to stab, hit, insult, rob or ravage the football pitch of any non-British citizen, as there are often local regulations strictly controlling such activities.

VALID FOR ALL EUROPEAN COMPETITIONS AND FOR THE WORLD CUP, IF BY SOME MIRACLE SCOTLAND QUALIFIES THIS TIME.

FOR RHODESIAN ATHLETES

Her Britannic Majesty's Principal Secretary of State for Foreign Affairs Requests and requires all those whom it may concern to understand fully that he had nothing to do with the issuing of this passport, and that at the slightest sign of protest you are welcome to confiscate it, but that on the other hand if nobody objects you might as well let the poor devil do his jumping and hurdling or whatever, after all we've got a lot of money tied up in Rhodesia and it's best to let sleeping dogs lie, we always say. Presentation of this passport at any British consulate entitles the bearer to 1 free sherry.

VISA FOR MOROCCAN COLONELS

BRITISH VISA

This visa entitles any Moroccan colonel seeking asylum, British justice and shelter in Gibraltar or any place whatsoever, to fly straight back to Morocco and be shot. There are economic and diplomatic reasons for this which you would not understand.

No Spikka da Scouse

... and with the Common Market, Italian workers will soon be settling around BILL TIDY

"No, no, lad . . . cock your little finger like this!"

"But Eddie, I got to pinch somebody!"

". . . and another thing, Vanucci. Just because you're a bloody communist, don't think you're getting my job!"

"Should be ashamed of yourself . . . you know he's not used to pints. Did you bring the cow heels for his breakfast?"

"Got to hand it to them eyeties. Giorgio could see Bertha with the boot polish and he still went in there!"

"'Ere . . . I've got a Mafia deduction too!"

"Tell me about Milan, Giorgio!"

"Can't work a full day, Mr. Grimley. Giorgio says it's the Festival of the Madonna of Macclesfield!"

"Do you mind, Signor. I am writing to my mother."

Heard from the Comte de Paris lately?
The Margrave of Erbach-Schönberg?
Appeal letters are attracting a better class
of signatory these days

Declined With Thanks

by BASIL BOOTHROYD

DEAR LORD HARLECH,

I was much touched by your letter of yesterday, and handsome leaflet offering me a commemorative two-handled European Movement mug at £94.50.

It naturally made me very proud to be singled out like this by a member of the aristocracy, especially when I see you've only got 500 of these mugs to unload, and must surely know that number of other people, mostly earls, equally deserving of this grand bargain offer.

I'd been out of touch with the upper crust for some time until a month or so ago. Though, about this time last year, I did have a very flattering letter from a Princess of Yugoslavia about a group of old Serbs, now based on Bayswater, who would be glad to hear from my humble commoner's cheque book. Otherwise nothing at all grand. Scout jamborees, church organ funds, lifeboats, coastline preservation, old folks' coal clubs and so on, all excellent causes as you'll agree, but, quite frankly, not one of the letters signed by anyone higher than an M.A. Even an impressively engraved invitation to an Albert Hall concert, I forget for what, saying that two Grand Tier boxes at £20 had actually been reserved for me, was only signed by Diana somebody, who could just have been an ordinary person.

Then, as I say, things took an upward curve a couple of months back with this letter from the Earl Marshal of England. Not that he pulled rank like that, just signed himself "Norfolk", but he took me right into his confidence about a new nature reserve he was starting. So that put me right on top of the world again. I think he made a mistake, myself, by enclosing a card for me to fill up, saying that I would/wouldn't see a representative of the scheme if he called at my home to collect a donation in person. Somehow, writing back to say I wouldn't seemed a bit blunt, but it wasn't clear who the representa-

tive might be, and in case it was the Earl Marshal himself, we wouldn't have felt—my wife and I, that this, particularly my wife—that we could have him here until we'd had the cracked toilet seat replaced, a thing that's been hanging over us, or rather standing behind us, for some time now: and where paying-out is concerned you have to respect the priorities. After all, visitors see the front gate first, and she says that until we get that back on its hinges, and some of the potholes in the path repaired, the seat will have to wait.

Then, again, I was a bit put off, over this, with the news that some "friend" of the scheme, and you can say that again, would fork out £50 or over for anything I forked out, of £50 or over, "to a maximum of £20,000". One naturally likes to help, and I might have run to a couple of quid, badly though we might have needed it at the time to get a power-point fixed that had fallen out of the wall in our master bedroom . . . but the idea that nothing under £50 would work this useful trick of doubling itself, making this new reserve comfortable for no end of ducks, blunted my liberal instincts. Given different circumstances, such as lower laundry and boot-repair costs, nothing would have pleased me more than to shoot off the maximum gift of £20,000, on condition that I could see the "friend's" face when the Earl Marshal called him up with the good news.

Still, this isn't a very polite way of answering your letter, brandishing a 16th duke at you, when you're only a 5th earl. I don't mean it like that. It's just that I thought you'd be interested in how other Debrett-type people go about the fund-raising business. What you want from me, obviously, is your handsome leaflet back, or at least the part of it that says:

Par la présente commande ferme, je désire recevoir . . . coupe(s)—

No, sorry. It was nice of you to send me

128

everything in two languages, in case I was French (I expect you've heard of the de Boothroyds?), though I must say it could be interpreted as fostering the French idea that they're the only people in the European Movement that matter, next, I mean, to the British . . . And I'm wondering, there, whether your leaflet was done in French first and put into English later. When you say about each mug being hand numbered as part of the inscription, "which details the limitation on the number produced", there's something funny about it, whereas the French version, "avec les détails de limitation de production", probably reads OK. Not that I personally give a *zut*. But will anyone else be offended? Like the Italians, say? At least you've given the prices in all our languages, including theirs: but it strikes me that a prospective client in the poorer parts of Naples, say, would want to know what sort of mug he was getting, or indeed being, for 137,498 lire. It's all right for us. We get your little history lesson, and everything (*Depuis 1945, le Mouvement pour l'Unité Européenne a fait des progrès tangibles . . .*). And I see you're even bringing in the Americans in the price list, at $245.00, on the basis of that good old special relationship, I suppose, and I'd be interested to know, though none of my business, just what top people you've picked out to receive the offer on that side, because with only 500 mugs to go at, once you get all the branches of the Kennedys, the Fords and the Rockefellers flooding in their application forms . . . you know? It's not as if you were limiting them to one apiece. As I was saying, when I dropped by mistake into the French bit:

This is a firm order for . . . cup(s)—. Except that, in my case, it isn't. I mean, I'd like to take a dozen. Please find enclosed cheque £1,134.

But I'm saving up for the increased butter prices and the rest. And I've got to help with finding that, whatever it is, three hundred million odd for the entrance fee.

It isn't that I think anybody's making a lot out of these mugs. In fact, I'm not sure that this isn't a part of my reason for not rushing you my £1,134 or £94.50. With ducks, old Serbs, and other causes on which I get approached by persons of rank, I can see some positive benefit at the other end. Granted I don't get any quid pro quo. No offer of a Serb or duck, post free and insurance paid, as with the mug. Even for my £20 boxes at the Albert Hall I was promised Mahler's 8th, and the Finchley Children's Music Group Choir. But with the mugs, I just don't know. There's nothing in your leaflet, in either language, saying where the profits, if any, will fall. It isn't as if the European Movement is scraping together some campaign funds to get us into Europe. Not now. We're in. Some anti-European movement, preparing to back Harold Wilson in his fight to get us out again, I could understand.

Can it be a pure uprush of altruistic feeling?

Lacking further information, I shall have to settle for that. In any case, I'm filing your kind and very flattering letter away in my Top People file, with others, equally glamorous though less personal, from various lords of the Gas Corporation, Electricity Generating Board, selected Life Assurance companies and Toilet Seat and Gate Fixing Consortiums, not to overlook—and how I wish I could—Her very own Majesty's Commissioners of Inland Revenue.

YOURS NOT KNOWING WHERE MY NEXT £94.50 MUG IS COMING FROM,

129

"I find it saves enormously on washing up."

*"Oh goody! Another diamond bracelet—what's in my
next parcel, Chivers?"*

Nothing Bu

*"Me too—I got 25% Stock in Bahamas and Unicorn
Development Corporation held in trust till 21. With
optional interest deposit relief."*

"*Honestly, Marjorie, I completely forgot that I gave you a boat last year too.*"

he Best by McMURTRY

"*Just how much money did you put in the Christmas pudding, Godfrey?*"

"I'd withhold my favours if I could remember what they were!"

Not the Only Pebble on the Beach

VINCENT MULCHRONE v. the Madding Crowd

Funny how you go off people. I've just gone off Charlie Chaplin and Oona. They've blown Evoia.

It's just a little Greek Island, barely known as a tourist haunt. But that's where they're going for their holiday. And if the discerning Chaplins have chosen it, can the travel brochures for a dozen half-finished hotels be far behind?

For some years now, Evoia has been the secret place for a friend of mine who is a travel writer. He has a couple of other quiet places stashed away, so he's not entirely destitute. But Charlie Chaplin has cut his private discoveries by about a third.

Considering their privileged position—free trips, and grog, and all—our travel writers are a remarkably honest bunch in my experience. But they are human, too. And part of their job is to steer the masses where *they* are not. They don't actually cheat. They simply write in a private language, clear as a bookie's tic-tac to each other, but unnoticed by the general public churning through acres of holiday supplements in early January.

You have to know your travel writer, of course, and even the nuances. "Quiet resort" could well mean they roll up the pavements, supposing they have pavements, at 9 p.m. "Quietly positioned" can generally be taken to mean that it's miles away from anywhere and the bus comes most Tuesdays. "Centrally situated" is a danger signal, because your balcony could overlook the all-night disco. Fine if you happen to be a disco fan who has rumbled the code.

Before we leave wunnerful Greece, take a sentence in a travel article going something like this: "Take the ferry which plies regularly from Piraeus, calling in at dear old Poros, then on to the gaiety of Hydra and the unique charms of Milos."

Now, which of those three islands do you suppose the writer prefers? You're right. It's Poros. He had to mention it because he loves it and spends holidays there. Privately he wouldn't spend more than a quick lunchtime among the pseudo-transatlantic artists who have turned Hydra into a caricature.

I was in Lloret de Mar in 1949 when the only other Englishman in the village was the present Speaker of the House of Commons. He didn't speak. Neither did I.

But if he was thinking what I was thinking, it was that the other wouldn't be so stupid as to spread the news at home that there existed a rough and ready, fantastically cheap stretch of the Spanish coast called the Costa Brava. Anyway, *I* didn't snitch.

Neither, generally speaking, do the travel writers. Some do private swops. One, with a lien on a £100 cottage on the undiscovered Costa del Tuppence, can bank on a colleague holding off for a while. Otherwise he just *could* write a piece about the Anatolian bay where the other gets his ouzo for a penny, b. and b. for 50p, *and* change out of a quid for the whole day. It may not be an exclusively British trait, but it is a fact that, when it comes to holidays, the rich and the poor tend to stick together—that is, the rich with the rich, and the poor with the poor.

The rich go to the length of building stockades around their mini-villages in the West Indies. They may not know much about the West Indies, but at least a chap knows whose wife he's bathing with. Travel writers steer clear.

At the other end of the scale, among the package tours, they perform a

"*He was a dreadful hypochondriac.*"

*"Poor Thompson, he's terribly afraid that the permissive age
will pass him by."*

"Where do I go to get stripped?"

valuable service if only in advising people not to book into an hotel which appears in the travel brochure as an "artist's impression."

Occasionally they slip up, like the rest of us. I once found myself in an hotel in Ibiza which was unfinished and practically unstaffed. Well recommended by several travel writers who hadn't been there, its lifts were still being installed. The only happy couple there were honeymooners who gladly ran up six flights of stairs. The putative foyer shook with the protests of the one-legged, middle-aged, Englishman who had long since lost the urge for speed but still wanted to get to his bed on the fourth floor without doing himself a damage.

The travel writers, as I say, have the advantage of most of us because they get there first, and want to hug their new-found joy to themselves for a little while.

(Well, perhaps not first. That distinction goes to the cabin crews of the big jets who, given a two or three day rest period—known as "slipping"—anywhere around the main routes, go off at a tangent and find gloriously cheap spots which they enjoy and then abandon at first sight of a batch of blue-rinsed matrons from Decatur, Ala.)

One wonders what travel writers for foreign papers say about us? ("That's a deal then, Hank. I lay off Ullswater, and you lay off the East Coast until I get my cottage in Cleethorpes tied up").

It must be the sheer speed with which they "do" Yurrup that makes so many Americans fall victim to the "If it's Tuesday it *must* be Naples" syndrome. Ask the men who run the Thames pleasure boats. They say that confusion between the Tower of London and the Leaning Tower of Pisa is commonplace. And they're tired of being asked "When do we pass Notre Dame?"

Where the travel writers do send them is to Fleet Street, where they pack

"Can Sir Gilbert come out to play?"

into a hostelry called the Cheshire Cheese. There, on steamy August days, they tuck into the specialty of the house, steak and kidney pud. The sight is something of a tourist attraction in itself. I'd rate it a two-star eye-opener.

On behalf of these people—and tourism *is* our fourth biggest industry—there has been some pressure for *two* Changings of the Guard, even when the absence of the Royal Standard says she's not home. But the Army won't have it. And, as Lord Mancroft put it, "It's a palace—not the Palladium."

I believe my travel-writing chum when he says, "We know our class of readership, and try to steer them to the places that we feel would be right for them." And the power of their pens can be extraordinary.

Some years ago, the doyenne of the trade wrote to the effect that the South coast of Turkey and the West coast of Ireland were the last unspoiled coastlines in Europe. Immediately both, tourist-wise, took off.

I could have cut her throat, because I had "discovered" West Cork and was keeping quiet about it. Not so an ex-journalist friend, now a famous Labour MP, who extolled its beauties in a national daily.

I met him walking along the shore with a face as long as P. J. O'Sullivan's bar. "Wassup?" sez I. Wassup was that dozens of readers were begging for the exact location. He fought them off for weeks, telling them that Cork was full of lovely bays, and they should pick their own. But one reader persisted until the MP and amateur travel writer committed the cardinal sin of the craft. He told the reader exactly *where*.

"And guess what?" said this broken man. "When I got up this morning, this bugger's pitched his tent right alongside my caravan. He says he's always wanted to meet me. And t'bugger's staying a *fortnight.*"

There was nothing to say. We both turned to P. J. O'Sullivan's. It seemed the only way out.

What Jackie Onassis and I Want for Christmas

****

by STANLEY REYNOLDS

It could have been worse, you know. They could have photographed Ari Onassis in the altogether.

But to begin at the beginning.

The telephone rang and I stepped from the bath.

"Watch it, Stan baby," I told myself, "this is probably some kind of a lousy ruse. There's maybe a gross and a half of lousy paparazzi out there in the bushes just waiting to snap you in the buff, for gosh sakes."

On the telephone there was the usual snap, crackle, and pop, alternating with a voice-down-the-bottomless-abyss effect. The telephone people lay this on at no extra charge. It all has to do with maintaining your sacred right of privacy. Nevertheless, something was wrong. Some calls were actually getting through last week and so a band of telephone rapair men were encamped in the back garden brewing tea.

"Hey, chief," they say, coming to the door, "got any hot water?"

"Some more hot water, cock," they say three minutes later.

"A little more hot water, Jim," they say the next minute.

"Just fill it right up, squire."

Maybe they aren't from the telephone people. Maybe they are gynaecologists. Whatever they are, they weren't going to start "sirring" some fellow who is hanging around the house all day when he could be out doing a man's work squatting around in a back garden somewhere peering into a hole in the ground.

Meanwhile back on the phone there was this dull, metallic tapping like that sonar thing in all those submarine pictures where Clark Gable hits the chicken sailor and says, "This ain't no Sun'y school picnic, mush." Five days later I went out to the garage and found a letter from the Editor—our new postman is a great kidder and loves hiding our mail. The Editor said he tried to telephone but kept getting a submarine up in a Norwegian fjord somewhere, and wouldn't I write a piece for the Xmas number about now rich men like Aristotle Onassis can buy their wives all sorts of expensive gifts for Christmas but they can't buy them privacy.

Well, they could you know. They could just rent them a room in my place and let the world try to get in touch with them here.

But it's come to something, ain't it? One minute they're taking pictures of Jackie in her birthday suit. The next minute they're disturbing Martin Bormann in his jungle in Peru or somewhere.

"Guess who's going to get the blame for this!"

"Is that the best you can do for a second opinion?"

The business of the fully frontal Jackie Onassis, snapped while sunbathing on Ari's private Greek Island, then spread all over some Italian girlie mag, called *Playmen*—and how's that for an original title? Well, it shows you what a fix the rich are in these days. The paparazzi, those scurrying, enterprising Roman shutterbugs immortalised in *La Dolce Vita,* mounted a sort of commando raid on Ari's isle. Masquerading as skin divers, they managed to get within waterproof long range lens distance of the unwary Mrs. O.

Snap click and there she was, boosting the circulation of *Playmen* which is a mag nobody ever even heard of before and which is run by a woman—and how's that for Sisterhood! The lady editor paid 30,000 big ones for the snaps. Now anyone can have them for 2,000 quid.

The episode showed once again that the rich ain't safe no more. Remember poor rich Elizabeth Taylor, snapped unawares a while back by a telephoto lens while she sunbathed on some island somewhere, not fully naked but showing much more of Taylor than had ever been seen before. *Look how fat Liz Taylor has got, tee hee.* The picture caption ran something like that. *Jackie Kennedy Onassis in the skinny he he.* That's the aesthetic appeal of those pictures.

Here's Jackie, the former Chicago socialite Jacqueline Bouvier, wife of the richest man in the world, widow of the youngest and most glamorous ever American President and I can see her bum *hee hee.*

Jackie, so they said, married Ari because he was the only man in the world who could give her protection from the world and the world's prying eyes. But it just ain't so. The world found the keyhole.

And isn't it a kind of a wonderful thing in a way that Man can go to the Moon and back and do long division and learn how to make woven soya bean protein taste good and still retain the innocence that allows everybody to go *tee hee* at the sight of the famous lady caught unawares, snapped in the altogether?

It's the modern, permissive variation of the fairy story about the King's new suit of clothes.

The rich can buy each other the biggest diamonds in the world, diamonds as big as the Ritz Hotel like Ari buys for Jackie and Richard buys for Liz. But remember in the Scott Fitzgerald story how aviators kept flying over the diamond mountain as big as the Ritz and had to be shot down in case they told the world and the diamond as big as the Ritz Hotel wouldn't be private any more? They can buy each other private islands and ocean-going yachts. But somehow they can't put privacy in the Christmas stocking.

It's the thing you and I have that they don't have and can never get unless they stop being what they are and become something else. "Money," the comedian says, it "can't buy everything. It can't buy poverty." And anomymity, too.

Howard Hughes thought he had discovered the secret. He hired the biggest public relations firm, the largest press agent in the world, just to keep his name out of the newspapers. When a newspaperman came along to do a story about the famous aviator, the rich billionaire and lover of beautiful women—Liz Taylor was the only girl to tell Howard Hughes No, and how's that for privacy when a fellow like me knows all about your sex life?—when a newspaperman came around to do a story, they gave him free trips on Howard Hughes's airlines and all the free drinks in the world, and then they would slip the newspaperman the word—No story.

Even that didn't work. A fellow went out and made the Howard Hughes story up. If he had authorised the biography it wouldn't have got half the mileage the fake did.

Howard Hughes sold TWA for 500 million dollars. His tool company in Texas had the patent on all the drills that drilled all the oil in the world. He bought himself the state of Nevada. He could buy himself anything for Christmas. But he couldn't go out of his own house. He was under house arrest. He couldn't open the windows and let up the blinds. *Snap click.*

They'd be out there. Waiting in the bushes.

Not long ago Jackie Kennedy Onassis came to London and went unnoticed. She sat at London airport in dark glasses going unnoticed except for the photographer who was taking pictures of her going unnoticed at London airport. That's a totally new angle on this privacy thing. Jane Fonda got the same treatment the other week. She was going unnoticed at London airport because Raquel Welch was getting all the cameras pointed at her—all, that is, except for the lenses which were recording that Jane Fonda was sitting going unnoticed just like any other ordinary passenger except no other ordinary passenger was getting photographed for the newspapers. In that league going unnoticed is getting your picture on page two.

A famous writer wrote a story about himself sitting in a room overlooking a football stadium.

"Come on," his cousin said to him, "let's go to the game."

"Listen," the writer, who was not yet famous then, said, "there are 60,000 people at that game. How many of them are going to be remembered in ten years time for going to a football game?" In ten years time the famous writer was hounded and photographed and interviewed and remembered so much he couldn't write any more and owed a quarter of a million dollars in back taxes. Nobody ever heard about the cousin. He's probably still going to football games.

How nice it is at Christmas time to be one of the little people and wallow in the luxury of anonymity with nothing in the bushes but the gas bill where the amusing new postman flung it. Safe in the bosom of your family, where the telephone may ring but nobody's going to get through. The boys out in the back garden will see to it that nobody disturbs their old pal, Jim, chief, cock. The only notoriety I ever achieved was in the third grade when someone chalked

STAN REYNOLDS AND CELIA COFFIN TRUE

all the way down Nonotuck Street to the corner of Jefferson and Liberty.

That's Jackie O's trouble. All that posh upbringing. They learned us early and different back there on Liberty Street.

*"This man is **not** Sir Anthony Babington. This man is an impostor. Replace his head."*

IRA PROVISIONALS (LTD)

ANNUAL REPORT

"A good year, despite all the money vanishing"

From the chairman's speech

Ladies and gentlemen, thank you for that round of applause which I appreciate wonderfully, thinking as I am that while you were clapping anyone might have made off with your wallet, seeing your two hands otherwise occupied. Which brings me to the main item, namely what sort of year have we had here at I R A Provisionals and where has all the money gone?

You will all have received copies of the company report unless they've been pulped down and flogged, and I don't think there is any one item on it to which I'll be drawing your particular attention except for the bit where it says "£50,000 was spent on the purchase of hand grenades". A printer's error has led to the omission of the second half of that sentence, which should end "but they never arrived as the dealer never got the money". We made inquiries into this and it would seem to be a slight misunderstanding, as Captain Flaherty who had the money was under the impression it was to be banked in Switzerland under his name. An appreciation of the late Captain Flaherty appears elsewhere.

Our policy of diversification continues to reap dividends, though not for you, and the idea of extending our investment area to banks, cinemas, cash vans and building societies has gone like a bomb, by which I mean it has actually worked. Profits before tax were £2½m and exactly the same after tax. They would have been more but that the little scheme we pioneered for making our own money misfired, on account of lending a genuine pound note to the engineer concerned for him to copy and never seeing him again.

Some of that £2½m has been reinvested. Our large fleet of vehicles is constantly needing repletion, but we have made considerable savings by acquiring vehicles that are just lying around with their owners apparently not wishing to make further use of them, also by eliminating much maintenance expense by disposing of the older vehicles. We have found that the most trouble-free method of disposal is blowing them up, as there's nothing more objectionable to my mind than just abandoning them in a lovely bit of countryside.

We have also invested in a new industrial side-line which has gone like a bomb, by which I mean it has blown up in our faces. That's by way of referring to the recycling of rubber bullets. The way we recycle them is this. We collect them and stamp them in big letters "The Irish Eraser Co. Ltd.", and then we sell them to schools. It grieves me to report that the bullets supplied by the British Army do not remove pencil marks.

So, out of that £2½m, we have spent wisely on car disposal and the purchase of a John Bull printing set. You will also see that we have earmarked a quarter of a million pounds under the heading of Sundries, and in order to forestall any questions from puzzled shareholders I should make it clear that this is the trade name for security devices, or maybe we can call them suspicious bulges, or not to be too allusive, things that go bang in the night. We have ordered fifty tons of Sundries from Libya, thirty-five crates of Sundries from Czechoslovakia and knocked off three rounds of Sundries from an English soldier who suddenly lost interest in life.

Well, now, a swift calculation will reveal that unless the John Bull printing set cost over £2m, there is still a profit of that amount to be accounted for. I will not deceive you. The printing set was donated by the son of Captain O'Donnell when he wasn't looking. Now, what we have done with the remainder of the money is this. We have initiated a personal incentive scheme. Now, what this means is this. Various people in the organisation have divided the £2m between them and done what they thought best with it. The policy has not yet had time to show fruit, but I can promise you that if any of those various people do not show a handsome advance on their investment, or at least bring the money back, they could find themselves at the wrong end of a Sundry.

So, it has been a very good year for some of us. We have had policy clashes, of course. Some quarters are in favour of our present policy of relying on Sundries. Some think we would be more effective with political methods. I myself have always been firmly on the side of Sundries, but I have begun to believe over the last year that there is at least something to be said for political methods. They're a damn sight cheaper. We will in due course let you know any change of policy. Meanwhile, in order to defray the cost of hiring the hall for this meeting, there will be a small collection. Right, you have five minutes to leave, and no-one who doesn't contribute gets out.

"What's your first reaction?"

Retreat to the Country

by THELWELL

"It says—overlooking National Trust property."

"... buying up property that should be occupied by land workers!"

"It's newly on the market. We only found it yesterday."

"Nearly there!"

"If you can get building permission it will be worth a fortune."

It's only me again

By WILLIAM DAVIS

SCENE: The Abraham Lincoln room at the White House. Busts of Abe and George Washington are on the President's left, the stars and stripes on his right, pictures of John Wayne and Ronald Reagan on the desk in front of him. Pat and Tricia are by his side, and the moving strains of America the Beautiful *are heard in the background as the President, choking back tears, addresses the camera:*

Pat, Tricia and I want to thank you most warmly for the wonderful letters you have sent us since I last appeared in your homes. We sat up until late last night, in this room where Abraham Lincoln spent so much of his time, and read every one. It's good to know that a man can count on so many friends in times of crisis. When I first discovered the cruel trick which fate had played upon me, Pat stroked my hair as we lay in bed and said, "Don't worry, Dick. You can rely on the American people. Just tell them how busy you were talking to Chairman Mao, seeing the Russians, and bringing the boys home from Vietnam. They know you can't do *everything*. Even a President has only two hands. Say it all happened while you weren't looking. They'll understand."

I turned to her, in that great bed where Washington spent so many restless nights, and said, "Pat, God bless you. God Bless America."

My enemies—people who have never forgiven me for bringing Alger Hiss to justice—say that I *must* have known. How could I? There are a million things to do every day. And Bob Haldeman always shut the door when he was on the telephone. When I asked him, once, about the reports in the press, he shrugged his shoulders and told me to get on with bombing Vietnam. He has a terrible temper and I didn't want to upset him, so I came back in here and ordered the Pentagon to smash Haiphong.

I never suspected that anything was wrong, even when I read that Bob was keeping $350,000 in his safe. With so many foreign visitors com-ing here all the time, one never knows when one might need a little extra cash in a hurry. And I don't have to tell you that $350,000 doesn't go very far these days.

A few weeks later I saw smoke coming from the room of another aide and was informed that he was burning files. Again, I saw no reason to be suspicious. Everyone knows that Pat likes to keep the White House tidy.

It has since been suggested that Mr. Haldeman may have used the money to buy silence from people who threatened to embarrass my administration. Well, he would not be the first man in American politics to apply a little monetary persuasion. Many of the Governors, Senators, Congressmen and Judges who now indulge in such

"I'll wait and see what 'Which?' says about them."

142

self-righteous anger would not have their jobs if they had not dipped into their pockets at the right moment. And how many Presidents, do you think, would have reached the White House without distributing the odd dollar here and there?

Some of the comments made abroad have been especially hypocritical. In Asia, Africa, South America and many parts of Europe bribery is a way of life. And most Governments wouldn't hesitate for one moment to shove these kind of things under the carpet. Could you see Mao telling his aides to give evidence before a Grand Jury? Or Leonid Breshnev allowing the Soviet press to attack him for silencing his opponents?

I want you to know that Pat and I haven't made a cent out of this job. I make a pretty good pay, but we don't run a Cadillac and Pat doesn't have more than a couple of mink coats. We have a place in California, and a bit of land in Florida, but we also have a mortgage and I tell you, frankly, there are days when we wonder where the next dollar is coming from.

One thing I should mention, because if I don't they'll probably be saying this about me too, we did get something—a gift—during the election campaign. A man down in Texas heard Pat on the radio say that she gets a bit lonely sometimes, when I'm away in Camp David brooding about the state of the world, and that she would like to have a cat. And believe it or not, the next day we got a message from the Post Office saying they had a package for us. We went down to get it. You know what it was? It was a little Siamese kitten, in a crate that he sent all the way from Texas. Honey colour, with cute little chocolate ears. And you know, Pat named it Abe, and I just want to say this right now, that regardless of what they say about it, we're going to keep it.

Some commentators claim to be confused by what I said last week about accepting full responsibility for the Watergate affair. I want to explain to you, the American people, just what I meant. I did *not* mean that I was responsible for the bugging, or for the fact that my boys were found out. It's not my fault that they behaved like a bunch of clumsy amateurs. What I meant is that, since I am President, I ought to do the manly and decent thing and take the rap for something which everyone knows perfectly well I didn't do, and which I certainly can't be blamed for.

It follows that there can be no question of my resignation or of impeachment. Let me say this: I don't believe that I ought to quit, because I'm not a quitter and, incidentally, Pat's not a quitter either. Besides, have you thought what would happen if I left? The job would go to Spiro Agnew.

Who, then, is to blame? I said last week that I would not place the blame on subordinates. I stand by that commitment. The fact that so many have either resigned, or been forced out, is solely due to my overriding desire to protect the Presidency. My former aides are fine, upstanding servants. Their resignation doesn't mean that they did anything wrong. It simply means that, with the press and Congress on my heels, *someone's* head had to roll—and it certainly wasn't going to be mine.

I believe in America. I believe in motherhood, apple pie, the Golden Gate, Frank Sinatra and Donald Duck. I believe in the Impossible Dream. This is why I say to you tonight: Forget Watergate. *Please.*

This sordid affair should not be allowed to overshadow the really big issues—soaring prices, the plight of the Indians, the energy crisis, racial discrimination. I am not to blame for them either, but I pledge to you, from this office, that I will do everything in my power to ensure that the guilty are brought to justice. I have today named John B. Halberstein III as the man who is going to do the job for me. He is a man of unimpeachable integrity and rigorously high principle, who can be relied on to keep his mouth shut and to resign if things don't work out.

In recent weeks the Watergate affair has claimed far too much of my own time and attention. I should be travelling around the world, providing the quality and wisdom of leadership which others so badly need. It is, as I said in my broadcast last week, the only hope for millions of people all over the world.

There is the Soviet Union, where our Communist friends have run desperately short of food. There is Italy, where they change Governments like you and I change our underwear. And there is Britain, where the militancy of labour unions is making life intolerable for Prime Minister Heath.

Earlier this evening Pat and I watched the movie *Patton,* which we have now seen eight or nine times. George Patton was a great American. He won the battle of the Bulge, when other Generals said it couldn't be done, because he had the will and determination to do what is right for America. Let me say this: I will do everything to be worthy of Patton, of Pat, of Tricia, of Spiro, of Congress, of the *New York Times* and *Washington Post,* and of all the wonderful, kind-hearted, generous people who elected me President.

Edward Kennedy had his Chappaquiddick. George McGovern had his Eagleton. I have Watergate. I ask for your prayers, just in case I need them. God bless each and everyone of you. And don't worry: you will still have Nixon to kick around some more.

THE WATER
Exclusive

We know that the Republicans had be
know that when they were caught they w
know till now is what was on the tap
to the Democra

look—things like : "10 Down : Five lines made
him famous (4)" ?
2nd : Lear.
1st : How's that ?
2nd : Must be Lear. Edward Lear, inventor of the limerick.
1st : By God, Joe, it fits ! How'd you like to run for President ?
2nd : No thanks, I firmly believe I would never be elected to
lead my country.
1st : But maybe the country would vote for a loser.
2nd : That's why we chose the Senator, remember ?
1st : Senator who ?

TAPE A

First man : Hey, Joe . . .
Second man : Yeah ?
1st : Did you see the Senator on TV last night ?
2nd : Senator who ?
1st : Senator McGovern, of course.
2nd : Oh, sure. Wasn't he great ? Fantastic, marvellous.
1st : Perfect. A knock-out. Can't fail.

Two minutes' pause
1st : What did you think of him ?
2nd : Terrible. I switched over to the late night movie after two
minutes.
1st : What was on ?
2nd : Edward G. Robinson in *Little Caesar.* He was great.
1st : Really ? Think we could get him to stand for President
instead ?
2nd : How could we ? He's dead.
1st : Well, that would give us a gimmick at least.
2nd : It's too late. The Senator has been nominated.
1st : Senator who ?
2nd : Senator McGovern.
1st : Sure, I remember now.

TAPE B *(Twenty Minutes Later)*

First man : Hey, Joe . . .
Second man : Yeah ?
1st : What's on the programme for today ?
2nd : Well, this afternoon we're concentrating on the States
that we think may vote for Nixon.
1st : How many is that ?
2nd : Forty-eight.
1st : And what are we doing about it ?
2nd : Sealing off the other States so no-one leaves.
1st : Makes sense. Then what ?
2nd : At six the Senator is coming in himself.
1st : Great ! Senator who ?
2nd : McGovern. We're going through the speech again.
We're not happy with the way he says : "I firmly believe
I shall be elected President."
1st : Why not ?
2nd : We don't like the way he touches wood when he says it.
What are *you* working on ?
1st : The *New York Times* crossword. Whoever set it has
got an IQ of 190.
2nd : Think he'd like to run for President for us ?
1st : You're crazy. How would you like to promote a guy who
goes around saying things like—hold on, let's have a

TAPE C *(An Hour Later)*

1st : I was thinking about the Election.
2nd : Dummy. We don't want you to think about the Election.
We just want you to vote.
1st : That's what I was thinking about. I was wondering
who to vote for.
2nd : You're not thinking of voting for Nixon ?
1st : Why not ? He's clean, he talks nicely and we wouldn't
have to waste public money moving his baggage out
of the White House.
2nd : I still fancy Edward Lear better.
1st : Who ?
2nd : The inventor of nonsense.
1st : Think we could get him to write speeches for the
Senator ?
2nd : No. He's dead.
1st : What a tragedy. And he looked so great and healthy
on TV last night.
2nd : Fantastic. Marvellous, a knock-out. Let's have a drink.

TAPE D *(One Minute Later)*

2nd : Ed, I've been thinking. If I *was* to run for President . . .
1st : Yeah ?
2nd : Would you vote for me ?
1st : Sure.

GATE TAPES
Transcripts

ing conversations in the Watergate. We
noving their bugging device. What we didn't
y had already made . . . So over now
u, last summer

2nd: That's great ! I'm almost neck and neck with the Senator already. Another drink ?

Tape E *(Three Minutes Later)*
1st: Senator who ?

TAPE F *(Half An Hour After)*
2nd: I have now decided to withdraw my decision to run for the White House. In all conscience, I do not feel it will leave me enough time to do the crossword as well.
1st: The nation respects your decision, Ed. Pass the Scotch.

Sound of a Door Opening
Third Man: Excuse me, gentlemen, I'm looking for . . .
1st: It's down the corridor and third on the right, and go easy on the paper because we're running out of funds.
3rd: No, I'm going to the speech conference.
2nd: Oh yeah, to iron out the Senator's speech.
3rd: You think it needs ironing out ?
1st: Not at all. Basically it's fantastic, a dream speech.
2nd: Deep down it's one of the all-time great speeches. There's just one thing.
3rd: What ?
1st: We think he ought to play it for laughs.
2nd: I wouldn't say that. I'd just change the bit where he says "I firmly believe I will become the next President."
3rd: What would you change it to ?
2nd: We think it ought to read : "Talking of which, did you hear the one about the Mexican priest and the busload of nuns ?".
3rd: Thank you, gentlemen. I will bear that in mind.

TAPE G *(Four Minutes Later)*
1st: What did he mean, *I will bear that in mind* ?
2nd: Are you thinking what I'm thinking ?
1st: I'm thinking I may have seen that face before.

2nd: That was no face, that was the Senator.
1st: Oh.

TAPE H *(Ten Minutes Later)*
1st: Why are you staring at the telephone like that ?
2nd: I'm not staring at the telephone. I'm staring at the little gadget taped to the telephone.
1st: It's only a bugging device.
2nd: But who would want to bug us ? We don't know anything.
1st: The FBI ? CIA ? NBC ? Your wife ?
2nd: I tell you who—the Senator ! He's checking on our loyalty !
1st: Good God. We'd better reassure him. Make a phone call to your mother.
2nd: But she . . .
1st: Phone your mother !
2nd: OK.

Sounds of a phone being dialled
2nd: Hello, mother. I just called to say that everything's wonderful and the Senator is sweeping to a landslide victory.
Mother: But Joe, last night I distinctly heard you say . . .
2nd: Shut up, mother . . .

Sound of phone being replaced

TAPE I *(An Hour Later)*
1st: "Chapter One. The Senator Makes His First Mistake."
2nd: What's that ?
1st: It's the opening of my book, "The Failure of a Candidate." It's the heart-chilling story of a Senator who comes roaring out of Miami to take on Richard Nixon at his own game and never even finds a vice-presidential candidate, and it's going to be published at Christmas just in time for the White House to buy a few thousand copies. What's your book going to be called ?
2nd: I'm not writing a book.
1st: *You're not writing a book ?*
2nd: No. I've been thinking about that bugging device. Whoever's listening knows we have nothing worth saying. So they're going to come and take it elsewhere. So I'm going to stick around and see who they are.
1st: You're crazy. Bugging isn't news any more.
2nd: Think so ? I'll wager that people will still be talking about the Watergate when they've forgotten about the Senator.
1st: Senator who ?
2nd: See what I mean ?

MILES KINGTON

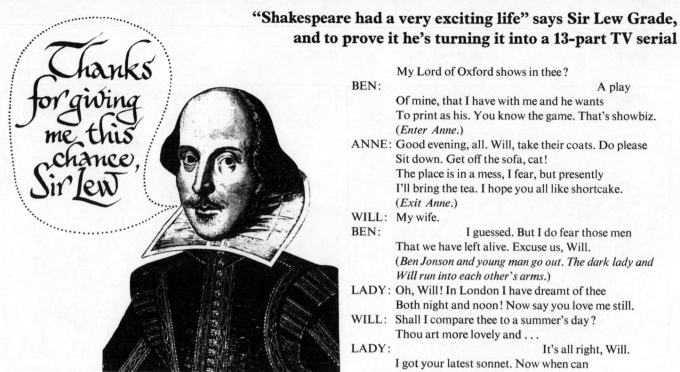

Thanks for giving me this chance, Sir Lew

Anne Hathaway's cottage. It is evening; Will Shakespeare is writing in one corner. Anne finishes a cup of tea, and sighs.

ANNE: It fairly does you good, it does. There's naught
In all the whole wide world like good hot tea.
Another cup?

WILL: Another cup? Another cup!?
The heroes of the globe infest my brain,
All crying to be set down on this paper,
And thou prat'st here of tea!

ANNE: You'd rather not, then?
I think I will myself. It's turning sharpish.

WILL: God send me from this marsh of shallow thought,
This empty wife, this two-legged commonplace!
But let my words hit home in London town
And I shall leave this dump.

ANNE: How goes the script?
I hope it has a story and some love—
I don't much care for sex and violence.

WILL: Methinks my tale will please you well, my dear.
It treateth of a noble and his wife.
(*Aside*) If she did know that he is big and black,
And kills his wife in bed full long and slow,
She'd throw a fit. (*Aloud*) Perchance I have not said
That late tonight some friends may come?

ANNE: That's nice.
I always said you needed company.
It does you good to talk. I'll put the pot on
Bye and bye. A plate of biscuits too.
Then we'll be comfy.

WILL: Dear gods and little fish!
If my wife was to Prince Othello wed,
He'd strangle her before Act One was done.
(*Noises outside of shooting, cries, swearing and bangs.*)

ANNE: That'll be them now. I'll get the tray.
(*She leaves. Enter Ben Jonson with dark lady and young man.*)

BEN: To arms, dear Will! The Earl of Oxford's men
Do press us hard with sword and gun, and we
Shall need your stout right arm. So rouse yourself!
(*Four armed men enter. After a swift fight Will stabs one, Ben Jonson kills a second and the other two flee. They throw the bodies out.*)

WILL: Canst tell me, Ben, what sort of pressing interest
My Lord of Oxford shows in thee?

BEN: A play
Of mine, that I have with me and he wants
To print as his. You know the game. That's showbiz.
(*Enter Anne.*)

ANNE: Good evening, all. Will, take their coats. Do please
Sit down. Get off the sofa, cat!
The place is in a mess, I fear, but presently
I'll bring the tea. I hope you all like shortcake.
(*Exit Anne.*)

WILL: My wife.

BEN: I guessed. But I do fear those men
That we have left alive. Excuse us, Will.
(*Ben Jonson and young man go out. The dark lady and Will run into each other's arms.*)

LADY: Oh, Will! In London I have dreamt of thee
Both night and noon! Now say you love me still.

WILL: Shall I compare thee to a summer's day?
Thou art more lovely and . . .

LADY: It's all right, Will.
I got your latest sonnet. Now when can
You come to London?

WILL: When I've sold a script.
I send them every day such tales of kings,
Of Scottish madmen, Danish nincompoops,
That soon they're bound to buy. Then I'll be there.
But tell me, love, who's that young blade with Ben?

LADY: Oh, just a friend.

WILL: You're sure?

LADY: Of course I am!
I've know young W.H. since he was nine,
And anyway he's not like that. He's queer.

WILL: What! Him and Ben?

LADY: I think so once.

WILL: He's nice.
(*Dark Lady looks at him sharply. Enter Anne.*)

ANNE: Well, I'll be mother. You like two lumps and milk?
(*Enter Ben Jonson and Mr. W.H.*)
I hope you found the place. It's difficult
To see the outside privy in the dark.

BEN: I almost quite forgot. I have a letter
Sent to thee by Burbage, who dost say
All sorts of nice things on thy latest script.

WILL: Hot dog! Let's look. (*He opens and reads letter.*)
Willst get a load of this!
He likes my Henry V so much he wants
To make a series on it. Part One, Part Two,
And so on.

BEN: Great news! Come back to London with us.

LADY: Where we shall have such times as ne'er you saw.

YOUNG
MAN: And I shall let you meet my friends.

BEN: Get you.

WILL: I'll come with you! Why, I did never know,
Until this opening episode, that I
Could ever lead a very exciting life!

ANNE: You'll need your winter woollies, then, and vests.
But I'll need time to iron and starch your ruffs.

WILL: I'll send for them from London. Meanwhile, get stuffed.
(*He leaves arm in arm with dark lady and Mr. W.H., Ben Jonson bringing up the rear. Outside, shots, cheers, hooves, singing and then silence.*)

ANNE: Oh dear, they left their tea. I'll iron his tights.
I suppose he'll be all right. Let's hope he writes.
(*She draws the curtains and pours herself a cup of tea.*)

"It's not often you'll find somebody who'll give you the very clothes off their back . . ."

Wonderful, darling

EAMMON ANDREWS comes clean

I. have a friend who, when confronted with a new-born baby by a drooling mother, eager to catch his comment as she unwraps her human prune, preserves his honesty and his sanity in one simple, shouted statement: "BOY, THAT'S A BABY!"

It works every time, except in my case when he said it about our second baby, forgetting it had already won him a large whiskey on the first.

It is not always as clear-cut—the route to escape from hypocritical committal. The new dress pirouetting before you will not settle for "Boy, that's a dress." The hair-do, the rhododendron, the fat man who believes he's taken off weight, the barber who has prepared you for Sing-Sing, the cook who has beaten eggs into rubberoid—all ravish you of your honesty, unless you be a man of steel or extraordinary far-seeing charity.

Backstage is, of course, the proverbial gravel-ridden testing-ground of honesty. How on earth can people murmur, "You were wonderful, darling," when no one beyond the sixth row knew that the actor was alive, and those in the front six assumed he was suffering from some kind of semi-audible St. Vitus's Dance? How can you murmur the "Darling" bit? But, on the other hand, how damn well can you not? Besides which, what on earth good can you possibly do by telling the actor he was bloody awful, unless you happen to be the guy who put up the money, or the actress who couldn't hear her cues?

So, what great sin is committed by murmuring "Wonderful, wonderful."

None at all, I suppose, except that when you do say "Wonderful" and mean it, you have by now so debased the coinage of the word, that you find yourself flying into a hyperbole that rings so false in everyone's ears, especially your own, that no hole in hell is deep enough for your discomfit.

I suppose it would be easy to say that honesty only really matters in bigger things, and that little dishonesties butter the rubbing of human relationships and make life that much more bearable. I don't know. The sages say that, if you're dishonest in little things, you'll be dishonest in the big ones too. Al Capone probably told his grandmother she looked wonderful, when she was, in fact, blue in the face and raddled from bath-tub gin.

I know two of my friends who constantly destroy my confidence in them by suddenly interpolating "To be honest with you." If I told them that I could then only assume that everything they had said before was a lie, they would be grievously offended, and take the biggest umbrage to hand.

However, backstage, boudoir or maternity home all take a back place, for the most perverted assault on our honesty was perpetrated in recent years by Her Majesty's Customs. What twisted searcher of men's souls dreamed up those notices that stare down into you at airports and seaports in this land of previously uninhibited travellers.

Nothing to declare, says the green notice. *Goods to declare,* says the red.

I have had—touch something—the happiest of relations with Customs and Excise men over the years. I've done the gabble declaration, in which I hope he won't really hear the word "camera" entwined in "socks for baby, pencils for children, soap for wife, souvenirs, key-rings, and a partly opened bottle of brandy." I have pointed out that the box of

"We're to keep an eagle eye open for a prodigy!"

"Just say the word when you wish me to start thinking."

cigars was a present, pressed upon me by an affectionate uncle, and that I didn't really want them anyway, but didn't like to hurt him. I have gone through the whole gamut, looking him straight in the eye and hoping he won't notice the little bead of sweat beginning to tickle underneath my nose.

This has happened only on holiday returns. Otherwise, my briefcase trips require no declaration; and somehow there used to be a great savouring of stiff, dry upper lip honesty on looking some cool Customs man straight in the moustache and saying "Nothing to declare." Now all that is gone. Now I shrivel past the *"Nothing to declare"* notice with my honesty in tatters, my pride in shreds, my nerves jangling, ready to burst out in indignation if anyone dares stop me to check that I have, in fact, read all the notices correctly.

In the old days, no matter what I was carrying, I went through Customs like an honest man. Today, I sidle by the Green Notice and, eyes downcast, crab-walk past the officers, like a thief with sticky jam on his fingers.

In the long run, of course, the only thing that keeps the world alive is honesty. Personal relationships break down for the want of it. Businesses wither for the lack of it. Countries crumble into disaster when it is missing from the fabric of their society. George Washington did it with his little axe and, thank God, he said so. It may not have saved the cherry tree but it may have saved a lot of cherries from going sour. The appalling multi-coloured dishonesty in international relations, the three-faced wheeling and dealing at the United Nations would send the whole world up in smoke if there wasn't still somebody where in one last corridor saying to his opposite number:

"Look, old boy, I had to say what I said, but the *fact* of the matter is . . ."

In many ways, this is what all the demonstrations and the blow-ups around the world have been about. The kids (who are no longer kids) got weary of the pantomime and wanted to hear the truth being spoken and honesty take its place instead of becoming a back-street commodity for anonymous back-street wheelers and dealers in stripped pants. People who

"Rolf Harris would have finished that two hours ago."

151

hoard information like scientists hoard pieces of the moon. People for whom the word Honesty is interchangeable with naivety.

Right down to the grass roots, don't be fooled by the hard-eyed guys who call you "boy scout" if you plump—even only verbally—for something as corny as truth. They need it just as much as you do. Even the godfathers of the fashionable Mafia need it. What their code-word for honesty is, I've no idea. But whatever it is, they need it.

One lie in a friendship can leave a mark for a lifetime. And, just before somebody calls me Malcolm O'Muggeridge, I'll stop and tell you a story.

Sid, the comedian, was walking down Charing Cross when he met Des O'Connor.

"Hiya, Des. Great to see ya! How are things?"

"The Crusades I could stand—it's these Siege of Acre reunions that really get me down."

"Great. Absolutely great. Fabulous season at the Palladium. Show in Las Vagas. Film coming up. New Television series. Absolutely terrific. How are things with you?"

"Couldn't be worse"—all the bonhomie gone out of Sid—"Haven't had a job for six months. I'm seriously thinking of quitting the business."

Whereupon, the ever-effervescent Des grasps him by the elbow, and, nose to nose, says earnestly:

"Sid, don't quit. Don't quit, Sid. I had it like that once and it all turned right. I've got a feeling about you. I've got a great *feeling* about you that you can make it. You can make the big time. You've got something. Don't quit."

Des turned and was gone into the crowds. Sid moved on and, three paces later bumped into (or vice versa) Harry Secombe.

"Hiya, Harry. Great to see you! How are things?"

Harry chuckled and tenored and giggled across the information that things were just great with him, and how were things with Sid?

"Couldn't be worse. Haven't had a job for six months. I'm seriously thinking of quitting the business."

Harry took Sid gently by the arm, and moved aside from the mainstream.

"Listen, Sid. There comes a time for honest speaking, and I've got to be honest with you. Sid, you're a good comedian, but not a great one. You could get a certain amount of work but you'll never, ever make the big time. I think you should quit. It's not fair on your wife, besides."

Meantime, Harry was taking a cheque book out of his inside pocket, flicking open a pen, and writing something on the cheque. He folded it and pushed it into Sid's hands.

"Sid. Do as I tell you. Open up a little shop. Open up a little shop, you and the missus. You used to know how to do it—and here's something to help you on."

The something was a cheque for five thousand quid. A last pat on the shoulder and Harry was gone in the crowds.

Sid got home.

"Any luck?" said the wife.

"No. Tried a dozen agents today. Nothing doing . . . but guess who I met today? Des O'Connor. Now, *there's* a nice guy."

Who are the Masters Now?

by GRAHAM

"The small ones inside, and the big one up here in front."

"Sorry to trouble you, but we can't find the red button we have to press before we can commence delivery."

"Mr. Miller, if the computer says you're seven thousand pounds overdrawn, you're seven thousand pounds overdrawn!"

"Oh, all right—the chef's speciality."

"We could make a start in October."

"I clearly said the lad would prefer a glass of milk!"

"Remember when he used to call?"

"I consider myself lucky to have a gardener even if he does have a bad back."

THE UNWORKABLES!

Outside the Knightsbridge branch of the Fynehoam Furnishing Co., stricken shoppers note that the price of occasional tables has risen overnight by eleven per cent. However, it is only their word against that of the mighty Fynehoam chain, since all earlier price tags have mysteriously disappeared. Desperate . . .

. . . their spokescouple, Mr & Mrs Norman Collinson, make contact with the dynamic new Government agency set up by tough, vigorous idealist E. Heath, Esq., lifelong fighter against corruption. Visited at 14a, Omdurman Crescent, Lewisham, by top agent Elliott Mess, the Collinsons are sworn in as undercover men . . .

. . . at the Alhambra Tea Room, Fulham Road, he is set upon by two thugs from the Household Basement and beaten senseless. He does not, however, reveal his identity, but passes himself off as a simple sideboard-fancier. Dissatisfied with this, Fynehoam introduce an unprincipled large-busted personnel manageress into . . .

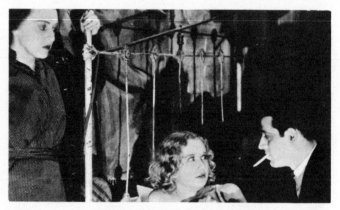

. . . Collinson's bed, with a view to eliciting his secret. Mrs Elfrida Collinson, however, becomes aware of the crowding on the mattress, and wakes just in time to warn her husband. The two Collinsons dress and threaten the manageress with exposure under the Sale Of Goods Act 1934 unless she agrees to infiltrate them into the premises of Fynehoam Furnishing, employed as . . .

. . . but, back at Fynehoam Furnishing, a tell-tale lipstick calculation on the Ladies' mirror leads the directors' hatchetmen down to the packing department, where they discover Elfrida Collinson distracting the happy-go-lucky packers while husband Norman goes through old COD receipts. Cornered, he flees, gunning . . .

. . . down the managing-director in the China Department, but finding himself suddenly trapped, his gun out of ammunition, his escape route barred by Sicilian commissionaires. Norman prepares to sell his life dearly (but at not more than 5% higher than he would have sold it for a year earlier) when the police . . .

Since the Government wishes to bring home to the country as forcibly as possible the need for both the freeze and its enforcers to be taken seriously, what better method than a good old-fashioned propaganda movie?

... *pledged to expose the rottenness of Fynehoam Furnishing and the board of directors whose self-seeking profiteering and open flouting of Government regulations threatens to pervade the entire furnishing trade and will, if allowed to range unchecked, bring society as we know it to its knees. It is ...*

... *dangerous work. In this scene, Norman Collinson, cunningly concealing his true identity, traps the sideboard buyer in his office and confronts him with the fact that a mock-Sheraton mahogany item has risen, in the space of three days, from £79.50 to £86.00. The buyer has Collinson followed, and ...*

... *helpers in Santa Claus's Grotto. It is while they are thus engaged that they are able to wander the store at will, checking accounts (they find that few accountants suspect gorillas of numeracy) and building up a vast and damning dossier on the activities of the villainous Fynehoam freezebusters ...*

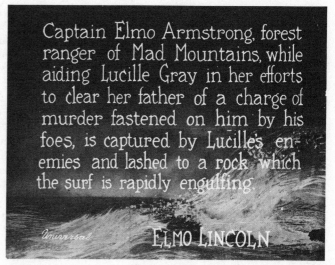

Captain Elmo Armstrong, forest ranger of Mad Mountains, while aiding Lucille Gray in her efforts to clear her father of a charge of murder fastened on him by his foes, is captured by Lucille's enemies and lashed to a rock which the surf is rapidly engulfing.

ELMO LINCOLN

... *meanwhile ...*

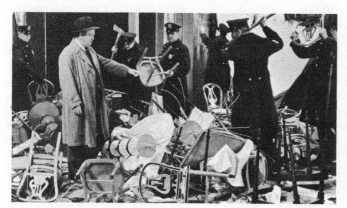

... *burst in and smash every item of overpriced furniture in the place. Standing amid the fragments of mahogany and ruined rosewood veneers, Elliott Mess declares roundly: "Let the lesson of the Fynehoam mob penetrate into the thinking of retail rats everywhere! Tangle with E. Heath, Esq., at your peril!" The ...*

... *board of directors is led away to begin a recommended-minimum thirty-year stretch, and Norman and Elfrida receive the MBE and a wonderful sunshine holiday for two on the fashionable Baltic Riviera for only thirty-nine gns inclusive (plus 10% due to the de facto devaluation of the floating pound).*

BRING DOWN TAXIS NOW!

ALAN BRIEN aspires to hire things

"I admit I've had it easy—I only wrote one play for the BBC, and they've been repeating it ever since."

158

You would think it must be easy to dominate a taxi driver. After all, except when it is good weather, or bad weather, late at night or in the rush hour, in Penge High Street or outside a metropolitan railway station, when you are so conspicuously dressed as to be embarrassing on foot, in Buckingham Palace garden-party topper or hairy slippers and a plastic pixie hood, when you are bleeding from some orifice, laden down with molten cheeses or melting ice creams or five kids on the verge of riot, or lost in a strange town or pursued by a gang of alien youths or have mislaid the Serbian word for "gynaecologist", when your feet are over-heated or your girl is cooling off or in any other emergency, after all, as I say, with very few exceptions, the taxi driver needs you more than you need him.

The taxi driver is a kind of prostitute on four wheels, the origin of the word "hack", randy for money, itching for business, desperate to get those figures ticking up, starved of conversation, bursting for a pee, riddled with superstitions, overloaded with prejudices, forever cruising, cruising, cruising, like the Flying Dutchman or Oscar Wilde, knowing that it will cost him more for each portion of a mile, or fraction of an hour, spent with his sign illuminated than it will you, with the light off, staring at the back of the driver's neck, fingering the change in your pocket, and picking your nose in solitude. You should be taking him for a ride. Instead, the universal experience of a cab passenger, is that, once the door is slammed, you are kidnapped. And so long as you are doing your porridge in his mobile cooler, it is difficult to keep your mind on anything but the ransom.

In 22 years of journalism, there has scarcely been a morning when I have not risen, promising myself—"today I shall use only public transport." But every day, for a journalist, at least for this journalist, today is always an exception. I start my appointments ten minutes late, and by the afternoon I am in danger of being a day behind. The taxi is my alibi and my excuse, my last chance and my first instinct—and anyway, it looks better on the expense sheet. Over the period, I think I have done almost every human activity inside a taxi which does not require main drainage. If peace really does have her victories, no less renowned than war, I should be dragging my left elbow across the parade ground, tilted by the weight of medals won in my campaigns with the taximeter cabriolet cavalry.

Nevertheless, it is never easy to establish that you are the rider and he is the horse. (The same, I've no doubt, goes for mounting horses, something, I'm glad to say, I have never done.) There was only once when, by a fluke, I instantly knew I was in absolute control of a licensed vehicle, and could indeed have ordered the cabby to take me to his leader, without either of us worrying about the fare.

It was in New York where every taximan regards himself as the eighth samurai. Those were the days before your jockey had barricaded himself in the front seat behind layers of bullet proof plastic like Eichmann on trial. Instead, the intimacy was as enforced and embarrassing as if you were being taken for a spin by a future father-in-law, and in much the same fashion you felt he was summing up your ethnic origin, your credit rating and your table manners long before he drew to a halt.

Jammed against your knee was his licence, bearing a photograph which inevitably bore no resemblance to him. Half the time it carried a super-scription announcing—"not valid unless the holder is wearing glasses." He never wore glasses. If the name on it was Anglo-Saxon, say "George Washington Churchill," then he was always black. If it was foreign, say "Christian Ewald von Kleist", then he was Brooklyn. Either way, take a few degrees of colour, he looked like Arnold Weinstock. And he began talking as soon as he scraped the bumper of the car ahead of you.

This one began by announcing—"You must be a Limey. From England, huh, I guess." I interrupted him there. "You're going to tell me you like Britishers," I prophesied. "And the reason you like Britishers is that you were a G.I. in Britain during the war, and everybody was just wonderful—right?" "Right," he said, grudging me the air space. "And the other, reason, you like

Britishers," I went on remorselessly, "is that your daughter, Sadie, married a Limey cop and now lives in Welwyn Garden City. And she has two kids, Sidney the elder and Rachel the younger." "Rachel's the first born," he muttered. "Say, you some kinda mind-reader?" "And you and your wife, I forget her name, are going to London to visit with them on June the, em, er, June the fifth. You've been saving for years and because you don't like flying you're going by sea. You've got some really cute gifts for the grand-children. Sidney, the elder, I mean the younger, is going to love the . . ."

He stopped the cab with a screech, partly brakes, mainly hysteria. "I can't stand it, Mac," he sobbed. "Is it E.S.P. or what?" I savoured the feeling of rolling another human being in my hand, like a marble. "Eliminate the impossible, as Sherlock Holmes once said, and what is left, however improbable, must be the truth. You picked me up at the same time at the same place last night and we had the same conversation. Only you were talking and I was listening. I never forget the back of a neck."

Of course, you can't win them all so neatly. But it is essential that you exert your superiority immediately. Get in before you speak—possession is nine points of taxi-man's lore, and he'd always rather drive you for an extra 20 minutes at the end of the journey than have to leave his seat at the beginning. Don't close your door until you are comfortable—a taxi with a door open is like a beetle on its back. Never show him an address written on the back of an envelope, the surest sign of the sucker the world over. Even if you have no common language, simply repeat the name of the most famous landmark within miles of your destination, however humble and obscure that is.

Only when you are well on your way, give him the full details. Once he's started, you're his investment and he's not going to be able to unload you without losing part of his price.

Take no notice of any complaints and objections he may make. Cabbies are not fools, but they seem to share a simple-minded, natural, instinctive approach to life. They are almost the last primitives, outside a BBC2 *Horizon* documentary, who actually scratch their heads when they're baffled, bite their nails when they're frustrated, and whistle when they're happy. However much

*"Why don't you ever do that for **me** any more?"*

of a nuisance and burden he thinks you are originally, within a mile he has grown accustomed to having you with him. Remember, you are the one with the money, and there is always an atavistic rivalry between taxi-men and policemen. If you suspect you might be over-charged stop him at a busy intersection, with a traffic jam building up behind you, and play it slow and dumb until the cop on point duty begins to stroll across.

Do not forget that taxi-drivers, who would seem to be the last disciples of free will in an increasingly regulated world, are usually apostles of pre-destination. They believe that fate has sent you, and only you, and specifically you, to try them. They cannot bear you to take the cab behind them on the rank, even though another customer is next to you in the line. Your relationship, so long as it lasts, is unique. And unlike almost all other providers of individual services, they want the enterprise to end up amicably, satisfactorily and profitably for both sides.

Taxi-drivers love to talk. No matter that the information they impart is out-of-date, inaccurate and barely proximate to what really goes on. Listen, why don't you? It is better to be bored than scalped. And most of the inside dope and reliable sources and public opinion you see quoted in your newspapers probably came from this same cabby who drove the visiting newspaper correspondent around yesterday.

Be reassured—he is not judging you by the standards he applies to his brother-in-law, and the man in his local bar. If he could afford to be driven around in cabs, he wouldn't be driving one. And if he were being driven around in one, he wouldn't put up with any nonsense from the driver. His attitude to you is partly envy, partly respect, partly condescension, partly avarice. It is not a bad formula for a seller to a buyer to adopt.

I dread to think of a world without taxis. It seems to me a kind of miracle that however backward and alien a country is, there will always be someone in the end who turns up to take you from one spot to another for a fee. So while never forgetting that you are the hirer, do not omit to carry out the duty which goes with your privilege and leave a tip slightly more than you think is reasonable. Try to think what you would have been willing to pay when you thought you would never find a taxi, and then halve it.

*"I'm worried about pollution—
they might do something
about it."*

The Sacred Mission of *Tori Priministri*

our perfect leader

S.McMurtry.

NOW is the time for you to hear th ancient wisdom of the Tori philosoph which finds its perfect form in the wor famous philosopher Tori Priministri. last you can find peace and calm in h creed of spiritual contemplation, whi teaches the unimportance of materi things.

"Why let your body dictate to you asks Tori Priministri. "Does your *so* need gas heating, or rail transport, ancillary hospital service? These a worldly pleasures which only bar th way to true happiness."

The wisdom of Tori Priministri is bas on the age-old writings of the East Ke Public Library. There it was revealed our leader, at an early age, that no mo than three books can be taken at o time. Pondering on this eternal truth, later came to other such basic beliefs for instance, that no human being permitted to write in the margin an that all things shall be returned after tw weeks. One day, with these sacre messages in his heart, he suddenly pe ceived the limited nature of the bo and the limitless possibilities of the so This led him to the philosophy of T

namely that all men are equal as long as they freely give up the right to material selfishness.

"Many men and women who do not have the time for perpetual contemplation have asked me how they can express Tori philosophy in their everyday life," smiles Tori Priministri. "To them I say—do not ask for more money. Do not absent yourself from your place of work. Rejoice when transport difficulties or lack of beef bring you face to face with human reality. Only by being content with the lot you were born with can you reach the state of Absolute Balance."

Absolute Balance, in Tori philosophy, is the blessed state of holiness in which that which one gives out (or Production) is equal to or with a bit of luck greater than that which one takes to one's home (Pay Packet). This was discovered by Tori Priministri in his early manhood when he attended the College of the Blessed Balliol. There he was taught their creed that only few are chosen. This after much meditation he rejected, believing instead that none are chosen, and that the only way to a happy life is by hard struggle through the three phases of wisdom.

with an inefficient sales force, computer problems and a suspicious wife?' That textile worker went back to his bench abashed, and resolved not to ask for more wealth. He had gained Absolute Balance."

Tori Priministri preaches a gospel of love and joy on utter frugality. He himself is a man much given to gaiety, though he often secludes himself for many days on the ocean where he meditates on the future of the world. Being a reincarnation of the prophets and a receptacle of the holy word, he is not allowed to marry; instead he devotes himself to his people, touring the country endlessly to bring them the message of self-denial.

Already many thousands have discovered the meaning of the Tori path to bliss, the Light at the end of the Tunnel. They can now perceive the Oneness of the Nation, beyond the barriers of wealth and possession. They are prepared, in the words of our perfect leader, to "sweat it out". Are *you*? Are you prepared to save the world the Tori way?

The Three Phases of Wisdom

PHASE ONE

In phase one a novice must agree to do without any material comfort he has not got already. Ideally, he should meditate in a small cold room, surrounded by such symbols of holiness as a dead gas fire and a non-functioning telephone. Indeed, many thousand of Tori Priministri's followers are making do without homes at all. By concentrating on the future state of Absolute Balance to come, a novice can already attain inklings of happiness. There will be temptations at first—visions of starving hospital staff, or unhappy coal-diggers—but these are delusions fostered by colour television.

PHASE TWO

Having mastered phase one, a novice is allowed to attain the state of V A T. This is really quite a simple mystical condition, applicable to all those whose annual holiness is equivalent in terres-

trial terms to £5,000, though there are also advantages to be gained by being registered for V A T under this limit (but see Vol. 3 of our simple handbook in 5 volumes—"The V A T and Visdom of the East"). Food prices will seem dearer, a common illusion brought about by increase in food prices.

PHASE THREE

The last stages in the advance towards Absolute Balance are brought about by the total absorption in the problems of others.

"There was once a textile worker," explains Tori Priministri, in one of the stories he likes to use to explain the truth, "who considered that his problems were greater than those of his master. So he went to his master and demanded more money. 'My son,' said the master, 'you think you have problems. How would *you* like to compete against superior Japanese products armed only

PEACE

LOVE

LIGHT

GRADUAL GROWTH

For more details write to the Sacred Mission, 10 Downing Street, London.

I have seen the future, and it hurts

by HANDELSMAN

This book tells you what your problem is! You are suffering from adaptive breakdown (a.b.).

The union is without issue, although your male daughter-in-law has two copies by a previous cell graft. (Getting used to it?)

. . . by the end of which, no one on Earth will be speaking Mawkish any more, but you have prepared for this by learning Gibberish during the return flight, while being served delicious Pseudo-Spinach by an almost human hostess. (Adapting?)

It's what happens when you suddenly find yourself in the future and you aren't even reconciled to the present.

To avoid a.b., you want to get used to things before they happen—like your son's wedding.

This need not bother you, since you can take a drug which enables you to simulate participation in *Come Dancing* in your own bed-sitting module . . .

. . . which, powered by biodegradable explosive corn flakes, is rocketing you to a six-day conference on Jupiter . . .

You return to friends and family, not necessarily your own, but people are interchangeable and disposable.

The future is, after all, a throwaway world. You can begin by throwing away this book.

Dear Mum, We'll Beat Old Adolf Ye

They're still finding Japanese soldiers of World War Two holding out in the Pacific. But have all British soldiers of those days given themselves up? E. S. TURNER is privileged to reproduce an astonishing human document.

9876543210 L/Cpl Brian Dudgeon
No. 134 Mobile Field Laundry RE
"Somewhere in Scotland"

Dear Mum,

It is well over 25 years since I last wrote, so I thought I would drop you a line to let you know how I am getting on (I shall be 56 tomorrow).

Mum, the first thing to say is that I have not surrendered. Up here in our mountain hideout nothing has changed since April 1945, when a bunch of us were dropped by Dakota to practise living off the land, ready for the invasion of Japan. Well, as you know, it worked out the other way round. Now the Little Yellow Men are everywhere. We saw two coachloads of them this morning, down in the valley, photographing bridges and culverts and everything in sight. Every second car is a Toyota or a Datsun, when it isn't a Volkswagen or a Fiat. The old Axis never had it so good, if you ask me. And of course we heard on the grapevine about the visit of Emperor Hirohito to his new satellite and how our puppet Prime Minister Heath was summoned forthwith to Tokyo.

There were twenty of us on the day we dropped and we joined up with some lads from No. 27 Airborne Packhorse Company RASC. A lot of deserters from an advanced blood bank tried to join us, but we soon saw them off. They wanted to take our washing machines and flog them on the Black Market, but we still have them all intact and bulled-up, ready for the Victory Parade some day. Unfortunately we couldn't stop the deserters eating all the packhorses.

Right from the start we have kept perfect discipline, with church parades every Sunday, thanks to our gallant Padre, who unfortunately was hit on the head during the drop by a crate of communion wine. Thank God he talked us out of cannibalism, which some of the lads were keen on, otherwise I should not be here to write this letter. It's been terribly hard at times to scrounge enough food, but the first ten years of bracken salad are the worst, I always say. Did you read about the rare osprey egg that was stolen? I nicked it, Mum, for a fry-up, and a dead loss it was, being almost ready to hatch out.

"*I don't mind the job but I hate the uniform.*"

166

"That's it, the commercials have finished."

Mustn't grumble too much, though. It's my belief we escape the worst of the Occupation up here. We have known all along how you people were suffering—how our American so-called allies sailed back home with the pick of our women, shipload after shipload (my Edith among them, I'll bet). We heard how Britain was being sold up piecemeal, just as Hitler threatened—how they tore up the railway lines everywhere, and shut down the coal mines, and sold off the *Queen* liners, and let the shipyards fall into ruin, and run down the Post Office, and devalued the currency and sold London Bridge. Not to mention scrapping all our battleships and aircraft carriers.

But what gives us courage, Mum, is to hear how the ordinary people of Britain are sabotaging the plans of one puppet Prime Minister after another. I mean, doing as little work as humanly possible, occupying the factories, blacking out the cities, letting the rubbish pile up and stink, defying the police. It's what the people of occupied Europe would have liked to do in 1940-45, but never dared! And the students are doing a rare job of subversion at the universities, from all we hear. (Must break off now, Mum, there are a couple of German hikers we are going to waylay—tomorrow the papers will say they fell down a ravine, ha! ha!)

Here I am again. The Padre I was telling you about took command of us when our own officer Captain Hay-Prestow was blown to bits trying to destroy some electricity pylons (the Scottish Nationalists get the blame for many of our exploits, ha! ha!). When the Padre leaves us on recce he wears assorted scraps of uniforms so as not to look too conspicuous, he says, in the city streets. Like all clergymen he is interested in railways and I shall never forget his face the day he told us that what was left of the LNER was being operated by men in German caps and uniforms. Or the day he reported that all traditional British money had been replaced overnight by almost worthless coins. He reckons religion has been pretty well put down everywhere except in Northern Ireland, and there were tears in his eyes when he told us how his old chums in dog-collars still belted out Evensong every tea-time to empty churches.

Fortunately we had a good supply of blanco when we landed, but it won't last for ever, and Sergeant-Major Drumbane is a worried man. He was 75 last week and is yearning for Chelsea Hospital. Three days ago we buried Lt.-Col. Walter Burbelow, Grenadier Guards, aged 102. He had fought with old Winston against the Fuzzy-Wuzzies and in 1940 they dug him out and made him a Senior Horticultural Officer, Scottish Command. We found him in 1950 lying in a cave, all alone, with a patch of dying lettuce, and took him on strength. He never stopped urging us to "Dig for Victory." Mum, he was a real gentleman. But talking of gentlemen, not all the Jerries are swine. It may surprise you to know we have one of them here as orderly, a quiet old geezer called Bormann, who says he fell out with Hitler's ideas.

The Padre won't let us listen to the radio. He says it is clearly in the hands of the enemy, because the news readers do not sound as if they know how to speak English. He keeps up a wall newspaper for us in the Education Cave and gives us talks on the British Way and Purpose from a couple of old Army pamphlets, all about the glorious Empire the jackals have snatched from us. Now and then when he returns from somewhere like Glasgow he brings us copies of the *Wizard* and *Hotspur* to raise our morale. They have strips showing British aces shooting down Huns and Eyties and Japs. The Padre says they are allowed to print fantasies of this kind because it serves as a safety valve. (Excuse me, again, but two of the lads who went Absent Without Leave have just returned in a terrible state of excitement.)

Back once more. The two lads I mentioned went into a cinema in Dundee hoping to see a Laurel and Hardy film. What they saw was a lot of naked nuns having an orgy. They are still under sedation, the lads, I mean. The Padre is hopping mad with them—they have already been in trouble for creeping up to crofts at night and watching television through the windows. It is deliberate policy under the Occupation, the Padre says, to corrupt public morals by all possible means and that is why no one is allowed to leave the camp area without a pass, which is hardly ever. As for me, I wouldn't know what to do with a 48-hour pass if I had one. Goodness knows I could eat a good square meal after a quarter of a century, but I hear all the restaurants are in the hands of the Italians, the Chinese and the Indians, and whatever I am, I'm no collaborator.

Later. We have just heard a rumour that Iceland is about to declare war on Britain. At my age I really do not see how I can be expected to take on any more aggressors, but I suppose there's nothing else to do but soldier on. The prospects of earning another stripe are not very rosy. What are *you* doing, Mum, to make life more difficult for the invaders? (It's really no good me asking, because you can't write back to tell me.) I reckon you must be pushing eighty now, but when the time comes I hope you will not hesitate to "take one with you." Stay out of the Common Market—the Padre says it's just a plot to remove the Queen from the Throne.

Well, it's been good to get this off my chest. None of us is supposed to write, because of security, and the Padre would award me Field Punishment No. 1 if he could read all this. I hope it won't be another 25 years before I take up my pen again.

Your loving (and undefeated) son,
BRIAN

HEADLINE PEOPLE

To-day there aren't so many. More and more
  Newspaper subs prefer elaboration:
One almost wonders what the text is for —
  The headline is sufficient explanation.

Now two-word headlines are in short supply;
  Even a three-word one is unexpected.
Though phrases that one can personify
  Do still occur; a few may be collected . . .

Man Held (a Swedish novelist, of course),
  Dawn Swoop, once more of all her mink bereft,
Gem Grab, that girl impatient for divorce,
  Those two Dutch crooks Van Holdup and Van Theft,

Old Wages Hitch, the county's last man in,
  With Rush Hour Chaos the Greek Anglophobe,
Trade Link, the U.N.'s most distinguished Finn,
  And the Viet-Cong commander Phone Tap Probe.

They seem a motley company, perhaps,
  Assembled thus in such restricted space;
But even so, personified by caps.,
  They're less upsetting than in lower case.

RICHARD MALLETT

Preachers should develop an "informal" and "conversational" style and not a "proclamatory" one, says a Church of England Council on Evangelism . . .

No, but seriously, I was reading in a book the other day about this bloke who went up a mountain to address a mass meeting and, as I understand it, what he was saying was that things'll turn out all right in the long run. And do you know, I think there's something in that. I mean, in my line of work, I quite often come across people who come up to me and say that they're poor, or meek, or hungry and I don't know what else, and, you know, I have to laugh. It's no use going on about it, is it? You have to make the best of it, look for the silver lining, I say.

Put it another way. Personally, and I'll be frank with you now, I go along with this feller I was telling you about when he says that there isn't much future in lighting a candle, say, and then hiding it under a bushel, you know what I mean? Mind you, I don't say it's easy. I should cocoa. In my job, I get to hear about quite a lot of persecution and reviling—you see it all the time these days, don't you?—people being trodden under the foot of man and all that sort of thing, and I can see their point of view. Certainly. But between ourselves, if you want my opinion, it's a waste of elbow doing anything by halves. I'll tell you. You want to start doing your own thing, like putting a gift up on the altar or something, just you go ahead.

You know, that reminds me. I was thinking the other day about adultery. Let's face it, we all do sometimes, don't we, it's only natural. But honestly, it isn't right. No, come on, it's not, is it? No, well this man in the book was saying, in his own words like, that it's not worth the risk. If you find you can't help yourself, he was saying, go and see your doctor and get your eyes or your right hand seen to. Best sorted out.

Listen, I'll tell you something else. I suppose all of us like a bit of cash and a few nice things about the place. But have you ever stopped to wonder why we bother? Seriously, have you? After all's said and done, you can't take it with you. Take something like the fowls of the air. You don't see them wasting their time going about collecting fancy stuff and stashing cash away. No, and when did you last see a miserable fowl of the air, tell me that. Well, there you are then. Same goes for lilies, that's another example of what I'm saying. There's nothing much fancy about lilies is there, but, well, if you stop to think, in its own way a thing like a lily is a pretty nice thing to be. You've no sweat, have you? So don't go worrying your heads about these things, that's what I say. You stick with higher things, like I'm telling you to, and you won't go far wrong in the end.

And another thing. Mind your language. I mean, if we all went about gossiping and casting aspersions on our neighbours, where would we be? You must have heard it. Such-a-body's got a mote in his eye. When all the time you've got a beam in your own. In a manner of speaking, you've got to clean up your own back yard. Look, I'll be straight with you. I'm not trying to pull anything. This man in the book I was mentioning earlier on, he says that if you'll just ask for what he's offering, he'll guarantee to see you right. Now, you can't say fairer than that.

So I'll just say this in conclusion. Mind who you talk to, there's plenty of sharp people around these days'll try and tell you different. Listen to some of those boys, and, well, it's like building your house on sand, if you get me picture. What I'm putting to you today is like a rock in comparison and that's the truth of it. Anyway, I can't go on talking like this all day, I shall have to be off. I hope you'll be able to join us again next week for another chat. Meanwhile, do us a favour and think on what I've said.

"Right, move up, you kids! We only have to collect M. le Curé and a pig—then home!"

Every French Home Should Have One

GEOFFREY DICKINSON
on the English au pair girl

"How many times have I told you children not to p[lay] with your food!"

"No—don't kill it, whatever it is! I'll get a pan and some garlic."

"You must have given him the '68 Nuits St. George—he thinks it's a terrible year."

I just said that I could hear a lark singing."

"There's something badly wrong with that child—he's only eaten five courses."

"My niece brought this from England—it fell off a counter in Marks and Spencer's."

"The usual, Georges—one Guinness, two whiskies, four Coca-Colas, two Schweppes tonics, and give the English girl a Pernod."

Ces Fous Anglais   By WILLIAM DAVIS

Continentals who visit Britain for the first time frequently express surprise that so few of us wear bowler hats.

The stereotype Englishman remains as firmly established in European minds as the traditional stage Frenchman or German remains in ours. Cold, aloof, sexless, puritanical—these are the kind of labels regularly tied to the Englishman's allegedly ubiquitous umbrella. To many Continental journalists, Sir Gerald Nabarro fits them to perfection; Enoch Powell is a close runner-up.

Many visitors think the British Isles are packed with eccentrics. They *want* to think so anyway. Like the Americans, European tourists are not interested in Mr. Heath's new Britain. They are much too wrapped up in their own problems to care whether we build modern factories and office blocks, or put a few millions more on the balance of payments. They wish us well—but if they care about anything at all it is the old Britain. They want to hear about Stonehenge, Stratford, the Tower of London, and the Royal Family.

Especially the Royal Family: Continental newspapers and magazines continue to give a quite extraordinary amount of coverage to every move. The castles, the clubs, the processions of Knights of the Garter, Eton and Harrow—this is the real world to millions of Europeans, not the grimy factory towns of the North or the impoverished valleys of Wales. It is one reason why Britons are invariably described as English, wherever they happen to come from. Continentals are genuinely astonished when someone points out that he's not English but Welsh.

Some British journalists have criticised Lord Montague for celebrating our entry into Europe with a vintage car rally to Brussels. They are wrong: this is exactly what the Continentals expected. They would now like to see more of the Queen (or Princess Anne) and less of Mr. Heath. And they would love to have Willy Brandt, or Georges Pompidou, dressed up in the flowing mantle and floppy hat of a Knight of the Garter. Tradition may have become a rather unfashionable word in Britain, but we are still regarded as Europe's leading suppliers of living history. Europe was not in the least surprised when the British Government created several hundred new Commanders of a non-existent British Empire on the day we officially joined the E.E.C. It's the kind of touch which other nations envy.

We are also, of course, the leading supplier of economic crises. They are widely regarded as part of our eccentricity, and Continentals enjoy them because (1) they are entertaining and (2) they make them feel better. Dr. Karl-Heinz Wocker, London correspondent of German radio and TV, said in a recent book that there are only two things people want from him: comedy and crises. Dotty Earls and Dukes are always welcome; his editors were delighted when they heard .that the Duke of Chesterfield's daughter could stand on her head for longer than anyone else in Britain and had become the official champion. Wocker and other journalists have firm instructions to look out for this kind of story—and, meantime, to produce a steady flow of proof that our trade unions have lost none of their taste, and talent, for pig-headed folly.

"Comprehende?—in this country we drive on the left side of the road."

de la Nougerede

Britain's labour troubles always make news on the Continent, especially if they revolve around tea breaks. It doesn't really matter that Continental countries, such as Italy, regularly outdo our own unions: British strikes are considered much more interesting. As Dr. Wocker says, it makes Continentals feel better. There is even a tendency, these days, to praise Britain for her alleged failures. Countries which have achieved a certain (and often superficial) degree of materialistic success are currently engaged in a weighty debate about "the quality of life". Americans and Japanese, especially, claim to be appalled by what fast economic growth has done to their countries. Britain earns their praise because we have not had much growth, because we are thought not to like hard work, and because we give the impression that we would rather play cricket than sell refrigerators to the Eskimos or bomb Vietnam. Americans flock to London because, as one New York author now resident here explained to me the other day, "we just love the decadence". Personally I have always thought that one was more likely to find it in Paris, but even Parisians insist that London is nowadays the more decadent of the two. A business

trip to Britain, I'm told, tends to attract as much ribald comment from office colleagues as business trips to Paris still do here.

Punch once suggested that the Government should build a British Disneyland somewhere near London; a vast conglomeration of castles, palaces and thatched cottages inhabited by beefeaters, mad Earls, pipers, serving wenches, and tea-drinking trade unionists. Tourists could make straight for this allurging paradise and ignore the rest. It's a pity the idea was not taken up: it could be a great success. Singapore, where I spent New Year's Eve, is well ahead of us in this respect. Having knocked down the Somerset Maugham world, and replaced it with modern hotels and shopping centres, the Government is re-creating it on a nearby island—complete with jungle villages, pirate caves and, no doubt, red-faced British colonels swigging pink gins.

One can, of course, appreciate Mr. Heath's reluctance to perpetuate the Ann Hathaway image. His Britain is supposed to be brisk, efficient, NEW. He would much rather have Continentals get their views from the *Financial Times* than from journals like *In Britain*, which regularly lists events like Blessing the Plough, Proclamation of the Beast Mart, and Tolling the Devil's Knell. Many Europeans do. Talk to a Continental businessman and he will tell you about the efficiency of the City, and say nice things about British technology. (He will also complain about British licensing hours: they are one tradition most Europeans feel they can do without.) Talk to a politician or diplomat and you are sure to hear about our "pragmatism". With two of the Common Market nations—Belgium and Holland—currently bereft of any sort of government, and Italy a vast political and bureaucratic mess, Britain's political system tends to be much admired. Most Continentals, needless to say, put it down to tradition.

Government-sponsored bodies like the Central Office of Information do their best to help. So does the BBC's Overseas Service at Bush House. Europeans are fed with a steady diet of production statistics and learned pamphlets on *Agricultural Research in Britain, The Motor Vehicle Industry in Britain,* and *The History of the Co-operative Movement in Britain.* There are give-away TV films on the City and Parliament, and taped radio programmes on anything from the Concorde to the Beatles.

The Beatles, actually were a blessing. They provided just the right mixture of youthful irreverence and British eccentricity. When John Lennon decided to protest against the war in Vietnam by spending three weeks in bed, Europeans everywhere shook their heads and muttered: "Ah, the crazy English". Carnaby Street, too, was effective. Here were the cold, aloof, sexless, puritanical English selling off Guards' uniforms and chamberpots decorated with the Union Jack—an altogether delightful touch of madness.

Alas, the Beatles have gone. John Lennon lives in New York, where his peculiar talents nowadays seem more readily appreciated than at home. Even Carnaby Street has lost its glamour: Continental visitors tend to find it tatty and listless. Liverpool no longer attracts much attention, and few Continental journalists ever bother to mention Manchester. The King's Road occasionally lives up to its carefully built image, but on the whole it seems to be going through one of its duller periods. Whatever Parisians may think, we have ceased to swing.

Indeed, there seems a real possibility that we have entered, or are about to enter, a new period of stuffiness. Some of the Continental papers see the Andy Warhol episode as proof that Britannia is reverting to type.

Writing in *Punch* two years ago, Pierre Daninos, creator of "Major Thompson", urged us not to change too much. "For me," he said, "it would be a sombre day if entry into the Common Market should modify your demeanour . . . In this world shrinking a little more every day, where one goes to Tahiti as one used to go to Naples, there is not one other nation susceptible to remove one from his usual habits, more than any of the Tuamotous, an ultra-civilised nation, whose customs remain more bizarre than that of the natives of Sunda Islands—yours, unique State in the world which allows one to feel out of the planet without leaving it. Stay that, stay what you are, and what you are not."

Some hope.

"They do grow up so fast!"

Caption Competition

A weekly contest in which readers are invited to supply up-to-date captions to some venerable cartoons.

"How much do you think we should leave?"

S. Rostron of Oxford

1909 caption.—Absent-minded Detective. *"Speak up, please!"*

"What do you mean, I haven't won this week's Caption Competition?"

J. von Achten of Hadfield, Cheshire

1921 caption.—*Seaside House Agent (to applicant for furnished house): "You don't mean to say you've got children?"*

"They're too small, George—throw them back!"

J. Sparry of Wall Heath, Staffs.

1934 caption.—*"A pair of trousers, Lilian!" "Anything in the pockets?"*

"Personally, I don't think it was a ticket collector in the other carriage."

I. Harris of London W4

1937 caption.—*"Oh yes, I'd always give up my seat to a lady—if one ever succeeded in fighting her way in."*

THE STATUS QUO CONTEMPLATES A POSSIBLE MOVE

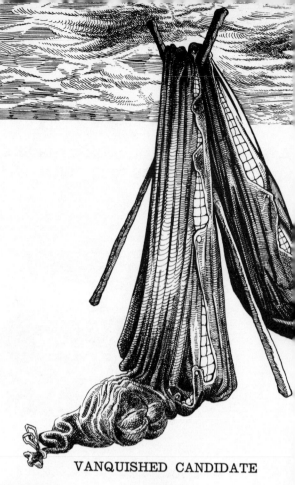

VANQUISHED CANDIDATE

BODIES POLITIC, USA

THE CANDIDATE HEDGES HIS BET   PARTY DOGMATIST

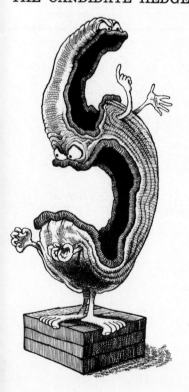

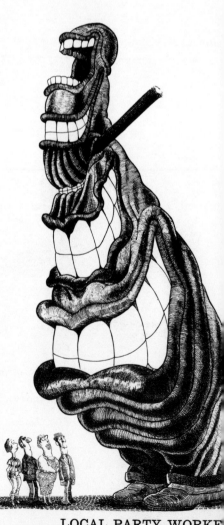

LOCAL PARTY WORKE
WELCOME A MORALE BOO

by JENSEN

THE SILENT MAJORITY IN CHORUS

TOURING IMAGE

ADHOCISM

The re-using of old rubbish is, apparently, going to be the trend for the seventies. These drawings were done on old paper bags by HONEYSETT, using a No. 6 wood screw and water from the Grand Union Canal.

"No, don't sit there—that's the ash tray."

"Shall I start carving the joint now, dear?"

"Harry! I left the groceries in that."

"*Where do you put your coal, then?*"

"*It's lovely, but we already have a tin opener.*"

"*Shall we have tea in here? I can't move the tea trolley.*"

"*I think I liked it better in the shed.*"

JEEVES SUPERSTAR

The same two writers who turned Jesus Christ into a modern superstar are now turning their attention to Jeeves...

(Morning in Bertie Wooster's penthouse flat off Piccadilly. There is a huddled shape in the bed, emitting occasional snores. Jeeves floats in with a tray and lays it on the table while he goes to open the curtains. The light floods in.)

Jeeves: Good morning, sir, I have brought your coffee, your macrobiotic roll and the latest Private Eye. According to the BBC, the weather outlook is a real gas and the Home Secretary has screwed up his career. Will there be anything else?

(The shape in the bed does not respond, but the bathroom door opens and Bertie enters, wiping shaving cream from his earlobes. He is wearing only jeans.)

Bertie: Bung ho, Jeeves. Still got it in for the bally old government, have you?

Jeeves: One is never sure of the true facts, sir. What the country needs is an alternative radio system telling it like it is.

Bertie: I expect you're right, Jeeves. I leave you to deal with the jolly old, the hard, the— what's the word I'm looking for?

Jeeves: The nitty gritty, sir.

Bertie: That's the stuff. Ah, is this a noggin of life-restoring coffee my optic nerves see before them?

Jeeves: The mind-blowing bean itself, sir. *(He glances curiously from Bertie to the bed and back again.)*

Bertie: I see you have spied an alien form ensconced in the master's bed. Does the name Susanna Steppes-Chantly ring a bell?

Jeeves: No, sir. Am I to take it that you and she have now shacked up together?

Bertie: Jeeves! Nothing like that at all. She is the beloved fiancée of my dear friend Tom Willoughby whom I visited last night. He was in a bad state—having fits and hallucinations and things—so I offered her a roof over her head here.

Jeeves: It sounds to me as if your friend was having a bad trip, sir.

Bertie: Eh? Well, if that was a bad trip, I personally in his position would have demanded my money back from the tour operators. Anyway, you won't find me getting embroiled in an affair of the heart with Susanna Steppes-Chantly, who is not only an egg-head of the first water but already affianced to the aforesaid Willoughby.

Jeeves: You're entitled to your bourgeois, emotional hang-ups, I'm sure, sir. Does this mean you are still *virgo intacta?*

Bertie: Bit early in the day for Latin tags, Jeeves. Try me again when the eyelids are working properly. Ah, do I spy a letter for me! *(He rips it open and lightly digests the contents. He sits down suddenly.)* Jeeves, the kiss of doom has just planted its footprints on me. My Aunt Dahlia has revived her plan to see me gainfully employed, and intends to call this morning, no doubt waving ICI application forms in her horny hand. I think the time has come for you to roll me one of your specials.

Jeeves: Right on, sir. *(At that moment, the doorbell rings.)* That may be her now, sir.

Bertie: Well, let's hope she mistakes Tom Willoughby's fiancée for an unmade bed or I'm in the potage du jour.

Jeeves: *(reappearing)* Mr. Thomas Willoughby to see you, sir.

Tom: *(tottering in)* Bertie, old boy. Mind if I lie down? *(He makes for the bed, but Bertie diverts him on to a sofa.)* Have you seen Susie anywhere? I seem to have lost her.

"Did you notice the Government warning?"

Bertie: Susie? Susie? Would I know her if I saw her?

Tom: Oh, for heaven's sake, Bertie. My financée.

Bertie: Congratulations, old fellow! This calls for a celebration. Have one of Jeeves's specials. *(Jeeves produces two hand-rolled cigarettes and passes them out.)* Don't know what he puts in them, but they make the troubles of the world go wonderful colours. What do you call them, Jeeves?

Jeeves: Joints, sir. It's an old Moroccan recipe.

Tom: Bertie, you're behaving very strangely today. I've been engaged to Susanna for three and a half years. You introduced us in the first place. And now you disclaim all knowledge.

Bertie: Oh, *that* Susie. I thought perhaps you'd got engaged to someone else, but were using the old name from sheer f of h.

Tom: Well, have you seen her?

Bertie: Have I seen her, Jeeves?

Jeeves: Out of sight, sir.

Bertie: There you are. I know you always believe Jeeves.

Tom: Well, all right then. But just remember, if you're up to any funny tricks, I'll break your neck and feed you to the RSPCA.

Bertie: I say!

Tom: Which brings me to my second question. Bertie, old friend and ally, you don't have a thousand pounds you aren't using this week, do you?

Bertie: What on earth do you want a thousand pounds for?

Tom: Well, you remember I told you I'm working in television now.

"*This rule about keeping their windows closed is upsetting the balance of nature.*"

Bertie: I do recall you saying something about a history of the Empire.

Tom: Oh, that. Someone else got there first.

Bertie: Then I want my five hundred back.

Tom: You'll get it *all* back, as soon as I've finished my new film. You see, the BBC is mad keen for documentaries on native tribes—can't get enough of 'em—and I know a man who's got this absolutely undiscovered pigmy colony somewhere in Africa. All I've got to do is make the film and we're rolling in it. I've got this producer with his tongue hanging out for it. Name of Maynard Chatterly.

Bertie: Sorry, Tom, nothing doing. No money. No thousand pounds. Not even a brand new penny to tide you over. And now, if you don't mind, I've got to cover the Wooster torso. Jeeves?

Jeeves: Would you prefer the Herbert Marcuse T-shirt today, sir, or your backwoods peer denim jacket? Personally I find the T-shirt very heavy.

Bertie: It is a bit, isn't it? I'll take the jacket then.

Susanna: *(yawning and sitting up)* Hello, Bertie dear. Oh, it's you, Tom. Whatever made you invite that man here, Bertie?

Bertie: That . . . ? But you're engaged to be married!

Susanna: Not after last night. He made a frightful spectacle of himself. All the king's wild horses wouldn't drag me to the altar now.

Tom: *(rising threateningly)* Bertie, am I to understand that my betrothed has spent the entire night in *your* bed?

Bertie: Now, look here Tom, it's quite . . .

Tom: Why, I'm going to break every bone in your puny little body. Stand still, blast you!

Bertie: About that thousand pounds, old boy . . .

Tom: What?

Bertie: Couldn't ask a corpse for a loan, could you? Mustn't tread on the golden goose before it's coughed up an egg.

Tom: *(indescisively)* Well . . .

(The door opens and in sweeps Aunt Dahlia.)

Dahlia: Bertie, I . . . Good heavens above! Why have you no clothes on? And what is that almost naked woman doing in your bed? An explanation please, Bertie.

Bertie: Well . . . you see, Aunt . . .

Jeeves: Perhaps I might explain, your Lady. Mr. Wooster had dug your letter very much and had decided to start work today. You blew in on his first session.

Dahlia: His first session as *what*, may I ask? A white slaver?

Jeeves: No, your Lady. A camera freak. He has followed the example of the Earl of Lichfield, another distinguished photographer. The lady on the bed is modelling a new nightgown.

Dahlia: Well, I suppose if it's all right for Lichfield . . . Who *is* the young lady, may I ask?

Susanna: I am Bertie's fiancée. We are to be married.

Bertie: Oh no we are not!

Susanna: Oh but, Bertie, after the sweet way you cared for me last night, and the foul way Tom treated me . . .

Bertie: This is Tom Willoughby, Aunt Dahlia, a friend of mine who goes around threatening

"I still say you tend to overfeed that budgie . . ."

people. This is Susanna Steppes-Chantly whom I am on no account going to marry. I think you know Jeeves.

Dahlia: If this is professional life, Bertie, I am having second thoughts about you having a job. *(The bell rings.)* Oh, Bertie, I hope you don't mind, I asked a friend of mine to meet me here. A very sweet man from the BBC called Maynard Chatterly. Do you know him?

Bertie: The name is vaguely . . .

Tom: My God! *(In an undertone)* I must have a word with you, Jeeves. This is the producer I was talking about. Well, I've got a confession. To convince him that I had the money for the film, I let him gain the impression that . . . well, that I was Bertram Wooster.

Jeeves: Far out, sir. You can leave it to me, sir. *(He exits.)*

Dahlia: Camera or no camera—and now that I think of it I see no camera—should we not get dressed to receive my friend?

Jeeves: *(returning)* I am afraid Mr. Chatterly has split in a hurry. I gathered he was making tracks for the BBC.

Dahlia: Damn and blast! *(She rushes out.)*

Tom: You'll let me have that thousand, won't you Bertie?

Bertie: Yes, yes.

Tom: Rightly-ho! *(He rushes out.)*

Susanna: *(dressing swiftly)* Oh, Bertie, you are such a good person. I'm sure we shall be very happy.

Bertie: I'm pretty happy already, thanks.

Susanna: And so modest. Bye bye! *(She leaves with a kiss which Bertie takes like a man.)*

Bertie: Well, Jeeves, I don't know how you got rid of that friend of Aunt Dahlia's.

Jeeves: Nothing to it, sir. I know a little of the minds of these media freaks. I hyped him that you were entertaining a certain TV critic. He turned green and fled.

Bertie: Dashed if I know what you're talking about half the time, Jeeves, but never mind. Now, what do we do about Susanna Hyphen-Whatsit?

Jeeves: It's already done, sir. I ventured to plant half a pound of hash about her person. I tipped off the fuzz by phone and she should get busted for six months or so. We won't see her before Christmas.

Bertie: There you go again, talking above my head. But as long as you've done the trick, that's all that matters.

Jeeves: Might I ask, sir, if I could take the afternoon off? I have been asked to chair a meeting of the Manservants' Angry Action Group.

Bertie: Still out to improve the world, eh?

Jeeves: Yes, sir. "I have seen the best minds of my generation, dragging themselves through the streets . . ."

Bertie: How's that?

Jeeves: Lines of the poet Ginsberg, sir. A not uninteresting American writer.

Bertie: You amaze me, Jeeves. You really amaze me. Well, pip, pip.

Jeeves: Right on, sir.

Victorian novels I read as a child are now published with lurid pictures on the cover. I keep feeling I must have missed something.

Judge Edie, quoted in The Observer

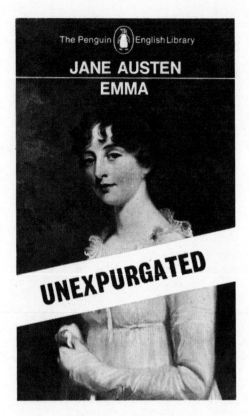

From: EMMA by Jane Austen

From: BARCHESTER TOWERS by Anthony Trollope

Her attention was now claimed by Mr Woodhouse, who being, according to his custom on such occasions, making the circle of his guests, and paying particular compliments to the ladies, was ending with her—and with all his mildest urbanity, said, "I am very sorry to hear, Miss Fairfax, of your being out this morning in the rain. Young ladies should take care of themselves. Young ladies are delicate plants. They should take care of their health and their complexions. My dear, did you change your stockings?"

"Yes, sir, I did indeed; and I am very much obliged by your kind solicitude about me."

"Pray, my dear Miss Fairfax, think nothing of it. It was merely that had you not so done yourself, I should have suggested we retire to the library where I should be more than grateful to oblige. I hate to think of those nasty wet things clinging to your firm young thighs."

"Mr Woodhouse, you are indeed kindness itself!"

The polite old gentleman smiled.

"Nonsense! I should be more than happy, Miss Fairfax, to rub down those shivering parts with a nice coarse towel I have brought in my porter-bag for just such an occasion. We should have that little bottom of yours restored to glowing health within a few short minutes. Do I perceive that your chest has not yet been rubbed in with embrocation? I thought not. Allow me, my dear Miss Fairfax, to . . ."

By this time, the walk in the rain had reached Mrs Elton, and her remonstrances now opened upon . . .

Mrs Quiverful immediately rose upon her feet, thinking it disrespectful to remain sitting while the wife of the bishop stood.

"Pray be seated, Mrs Quiverful, pray keep your seat! Your husband has been most weak and foolish. It is impossible, Mrs Quiverful, to help people who will not help themselves. I much fear that I can now do nothing for you in this matter."

"Oh! Mrs Proudie, don't say so," said the poor woman, again jumping up.

"*Pray* be seated, Mrs Quiverful! Your husband's folly is a continuing source of astonishment to the Bishop and myself: that a clergyman of our diocese should interest himself in the welfare of his choir is one thing; that he should form a company entitled Small Boys Limited for the purposes of shipping his little parishioners to Morocco, Egypt, Turkey, and such other areas of the unenlightened world where fresh Christians are at a premium, to serve what ends I know not, is quite another."

At these, it must be said, harsh words, Mrs Quiverful turned quite pale; not a word came from her, but the tears came streaming down her big coarse cheeks, on which the dust of August had left its traces. At last, she sobbed:

"We have so little money, Mrs Proudie. Fourteen children! It's hard for the children of a clergyman—barely bread, Mrs Proudie, barely bread, and fourteen children! And three of them black, to boot . . ."

From: THE OLD CURIOSITY SHOP
by Charles Dickens

"I'll tell you why I ask," rejoined Nell. "I lost some money last night—out of my own bedroom I am sure. Unless it was taken by somebody in jest—only in jest, dear grandfather, which would make me laugh heartily if I could but know it."

"Who would take money in jest?" returned the old man in a hurried manner. "Those who take money take it to keep."

"Then it was stolen out of my room, dear," said the child, whose last hope was destroyed by the manner of this reply.

"But is there no more, Nell?" said the old man, "no more anywhere? Was it all taken, every farthing of it, was there nothing left?"

"Nothing," replied the child.

"We must get more," said the old man, "we must earn it, Nell, hoard it up, scrape it together, come by it somehow. You'll have to take over the ten-to-midnight shift from Chinese Sadie."

"In addition to my afternoon stint, grandfather?"

"Well, child, now that Spotty Freda has refused to handle Laskars, how shall we make ends meet?"

"Har, har, har!"

"That was not a joke, dear Nell. Our dusky sailor friends have strange ways, which Spotty Freda was ever happy to oblige, until the incident of the parrot and the jam-jar. I fear that we may not be able to sustain the loss of their custom."

"But, grandfather, I have my own reputation to think of. It has taken me fourteen years to become the most famous vicar's little daughter in East India Dock Road. Am I to put all this at hazard now?"

The old gentleman sighed heavily at his till.

"Think of it as a new challenge, dearest Nell," he said. "It is not given to everyone to succeed in gumboots."

"Yes, grandfather," said little Nell . . .

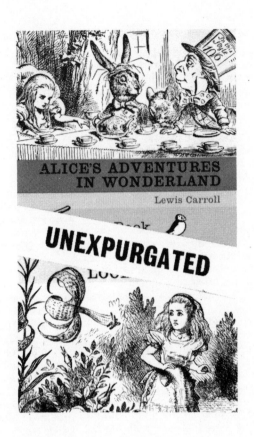

From: JANE EYRE by Charlotte Brontë

A splendid Midsummer shone over England: skies so pure, suns so radiant, as were then seen in long succession, seldom favour, even singly, our wave-girt land. It was as if a band of Italian days had come from the South, like a flock of glorious passenger birds, and lighted to rest them on the cliffs of Albion. The hay was all got in; the fields round Thornfield were green and shorn; the roads white and baked; the trees were in their dark prime.

I walked a while upon the terrace; but a subtle, well-known scent—that of a man—stole from some window; I saw the library casement open a hand-breadth; I glanced up.

"Why, Mr Rochester!" I exclaimed.

"Why not, Miss Eyre?" he enquired.

"But your breeches, Mr Rochester!" I cried.

"I have given them to the under-gardener, Miss Eyre," he said.

My eyes filled with tears. So handsome, and so generous withal!

"I thought you might come up, Miss Eyre," he murmured, "and play upon the spinet."

"A duet, perhaps?" I said.

"How nice!" he cried, pulling the curtains to with such rough vigour that a ring flew from the shining rod, "Miss Eyre, how exceedingly nice!"

From: ALICE'S ADVENTURES IN WONDERLAND by Lewis Carroll

And she kept on puzzling about it while the Mouse was speaking, so that her idea of the tale was something like this:—

```
        "Fury said to a
             mouse, That he
          met in the
       house,
    'Let us
       both go to
          bed: I will
    sock it to
      you. Come,
         I will not
            take no; We
         must both have
       a go: For
         really this
          morning I've
       nothing
    to do.'
       Said the
    mouse to the
      cur, 'Such a
          business,
            dear Sir,
               could not,
                 surely, be
              right. I
           am pledged
          to a rat'.
    Said the cur,
       'Bugger that,
          Let us both nip
       upstairs, and
    I'll slip
         you a
       ....'"
```

Country Life

Not everything that happens in Britain gets into the national press. This feature, to which readers contribute, presents some of the news which never made it.

Daventry's borough rat catcher is to get £7.45 from the Council to buy spectacles to replace a pair that fell off his nose as he looked down a rat hole.

(Eastern Daily Press)

After asking him not to wipe his face on the table cloth, a waiter in an Indian restaurant thought a customer was going to hit him so he smashed a plate over his head.

(Widnes Weekly News)

Mr. J. C. Bradley, defending, asked Sergeant Murphy why he and the police constable had asked for "Mr. Friedland" when they rang the door bell. Sergeant Murphy replied that the name "Friedland" was printed on the bell-push and they thought it was the defendant's name. They later learned it was the name of the bell manu-facturers.

(Solihull News)

She has advised them that if they find the snake, they should get hold of it by the neck and either smash it on the head or contact London Zoo.

(Evening Standard)

In order to defend the bridge across the River Stour at Bures, a concrete pillbox was built inside a shop on the Suffolk side of the river. As the Nazis stormed over from Essex, it was planned that the local Dad's Army or any regular troops about at the time would be in position in the shop. Part of the wooden facia of the shop would drop down on hinges and Hitler's men would be blasted off the bridge by an anti-tank gun in the pillbox. The pillbox was so well constructed it has made the shop useless for any pur-pose since.

(East Anglian Daily Times)

Chairman of the Bench, Mr. G. O. Williams, said: "It seems to us that when you have these migraines your thoughts turn immediately to wind-screen wipers." He said that Mr. Hicks did not consider the consider-able inconvenience he was causing.

(Monmouthshire Free Press)

Councillor McIver said: "I will get to the bottom of this one way or another. If there is any sort of wangle going on, I will blow the lid off it. This is just the tip of the iceberg as far as I am concerned. I have much more ammunition up my sleeve."

(Alloa Advertiser)

Helpringham has a unique claim to fame. Yoko Ono's false teeth box and King Freddie of Buganda's coffin were both made in the village's only fac-tory, R. Denny & Co. Ltd.

(Sleaford Standard)

Three new monks at the Good Shepherd Mission, Penge, are looking around for women's second-hand bicycles. They must be women's cycles because negotiating a cross-bar with robes on could prove diffi-cult, said Bishop Frederick Linale.

(Beckenham & Penge Advertiser)

Police officers who broke into a Bradford house found a 34-year-old Leeds man in bed with a drunken quail, Bradford magistrates were told today.

(Yorkshire Post)

Milkman Vallance Spridgeon (44) assaulted a man who he thought was having an affair with his wife, city magistrates were told on Friday. He told police: "I saw him in Eye while I was delivering milk. He gave me a sly look. I think it was because I was wearing my toupee."

(Peterborough Standard)

The winner of the hats and caps competition at the H.A.P.A. bazaar was Lucy Northway, not Denise Wheeler as we stated last week. Denise won the silly walks contest.

(Henley Standard)

Harwich Borough Council has agreed to call for a public enquiry on why 700 holes have been dug in Main Road over the past few years.

(East Anglian Times)

Doreen Irvin, a former prostitute known as 'Darling Doreen', who claims to have been both a drug addict and a witch and to have taken part in the exhumation of bodies for the worship of Satan, gave a talk to Young Wives at Maulden Baptist Church this week.

(Luton News)

"*Melvin here is one of our founder members.*"

186

x nuts from a Ginkgo Biloba tree
hich have come from China have
een presented to Aireborough Coun-
by a Guiseley man . . . Two years
o, he gave the Council eight similar
ts.

(Yorkshire Post)

orth Devon police are looking for a
opard skin which was recently
ted with a false tooth by a dentist.

(Western Times)

cots Guards piper Gordon Mackay's
ain journey from London to Edin-
urgh ended when police found him
cked in a lavatory with a greyhound.
nother toilet was found strewn with
opical fish and terrapins.

(The Scotsman)

otice is hereby given that "Horwell
aterbed & Watermattress Company
mited" has changed its name to
Momma's Frozen Products Limited."

(New Zealand Gazette)

fter a day in a factory with noisy
achinery and people rushing about,
ere's nothing quite like a peaceful
our or two spent in one's caviary.
here the only sounds are made by
e cavies. Their daily handful of
esh hay has a smell I find very
easing and the sight of the pigs
nning through the hay or enjoying a
ood tuck-in is very gratifying.

(Fur & Feather)

r. Morris said that the aim of his
epartment was to sweep away the
d idea of Worthing as a safe place
which the elderly could retire to
e out the rest of their lives in
eace. It was necessary to attract
e younger generation to the town.
r. Morris showed slides of some of
e recently completed buildings for
hich his department has been res-
onsible, including the crematorium.

(Worthing Herald)

oun. Mrs. G. M. Webster reported
at windows and toilets were broken.
chain with a marble handle had
een used as a weapon. It was agreed
leave the matter with the Pub-
city, Attractions and Bathing Pool
ommittee.

(Westmorland Gazette)

"He was in the hotel business . . ."

Mr. Jack Nutley, the much-travelled
Tonbridge railway porter, has returned
from a three-week conference in
Delhi dealing with the world-wide
problems of prostitution.

(Kent & Sussex Courier)

I've lived all my life in the country. I
was born and bred in Wantage and
for more than 40 years I worked for
the Pearl Assurance Company in the
area. So I know a cuckoo when I see
one.

(Oxford Mail)

An unsuccessful crocodile hunter read
an article in a magazine about people
making their own fifty-penny pieces
and "this set the seeds in his mind
and he started experimenting himself" in order to regain a lost inheri-
tance, Ipswich Crown Court heard
today.

(Ipswich Evening Star)

Mrs. Margaret Cripps at No. 19 was
not sure how high the water had
risen but it had come up to the eye-
brows of her garden gnomes earlier
in the morning.

(Harrow Observer)

"Right, Dobson—up you go."

187

Sheepy Parish Council has accepted a quotation for supplying an additional street lamp in Mill Lane, Sheepy Parva. At the same time, it was agreed not to have an additional street lamp in Ratcliffe Lane, Sheepy, owing to the high cost. There were renewed complaints concerning fishermen casting off the footpath into the lake at Sheepy. The clerk was given instructions to raise this matter at a higher level.

(Leicester Mercury)

Two people were treated for monkey bites in Bognor Regis during the summer season. This is one more than last year.

(Midhurst & Petworth Observer)

Bristol girl Vivian Rice (23) has signed her own peace treaty with the Indians —by marrying a member of the Flathead tribe in America. She is now Mrs. Vivian Rice Red Wing Nine Pipe, wife to Louie Nine Pipe, whose age is estimated at between 74 and 84 years. "It's rather like a fairy tale, don't you think?" Mrs. Nine Pipe said today.

(Bristol Evening Post)

When asked by police to give his name, a motorist said "My name is Nuff and I'm a fairy—fair enough." Staffordshire County Magistrates were told yesterday. He was banned from driving for a year, fined £30 and ordered to pay £30 costs.

(Staffordshire Sentinel)

The village hall at Wyre Piddle was crowded last week-end with visitors to an exhibition staged by the Women's Institute entitled "The Changing Face of Wyre Piddle."

(Evesham Journal)

Sigrid and Oliver were walking along the path leading from Cae Plan down to the beach on Saturday when Sigrid found the lower dentures and placed them on top of a low wall moving alongside the path. On Sunday, only a few yards further away, Oliver found the bottom set. They were accompanied by district nurse Miss Dilys Owen, of Noddfa, Llanbedrog.

(Caernarvon & Denbigh Herald)

"He's got the same personality as Spike Milligan, but without his sense of humour."

A 19-year-old Plumley man who had been celebrating in Northwich did not realise he had stolen a bicycle until he fell off it, Northwich magistrates were told last week.

(Northwich Guardian)

A Monmouthshire county-councillor was summoned by Royal Command to Windsor Great Park on Sunday to show the Emperor Haile Selassie how to work sheepdogs on horseback.

(South Wales Argus)

A Wisbech woman who stepped ba[ck] three paces and recited a nurse[ry] rhyme, as directed by someone wh[o] telephoned her at her home, co[n]tacted the police after deciding it wa[s] most unlikely the exercise had been [a] GPO test.

(Eastern Daily Pres[s]

The complete disregard shown by [a] section of the community for law a[nd] order was again highlighted by th[e] Provost on Monday when he spoke [of] cyclists still regularly using Colle[ge] Street despite the bollard placed ther[e].

(St. Andrews Citize[n]

welding engineer was accidentally
ed from a 16ft funfair cannon
sterday as he worked head-first
lfway down the barrel adjusting its
nge. He was hurled over a wall and
ft into a field.

(Walsall Observer)

told the Bench that the drunken-
ss case was the result of the morn-
g's hearing when he was said to
ve been pursued by a heart surgeon
ned with an imitation sub-machine
n and knuckle-duster (see page
ee).

(Brentford & Chiswick Times)

s. Cooke said that following dom-
tic trouble Mrs. Keogh and her
sband had separated, and he had
ne to live with his sister. On July
Mrs. Keogh went to see him, and
ile they were talking she pulled a
all potato from her handbag and
bbed him. Fortunately the injury
as not as serious as was at first
ought.

(Birkenhead News)

We regret that Mr. S. Krynicki of
Poland was wrongly named as Mr. T.
Blaj of Roumania in the caption to a
photograph of personalities at the
Fibre Building Board Federation's
annual dinner.

(Timber Trades Journal)

Police enquiries over twelve months
in East Herrington came to an end
when George Barnes was seen in
the early hours of the morning carrying a washing machine on his
shoulder.

(Newcastle Journal)

He told the bench last week: "I went
to Sutton police station to tell police a
stranger had called inquiring about
my brother's address. I was wary
because my brother was away and I
wanted the police to call at my
brother's house to check. But the
police seemed unwilling to check that
the stranger was not someone about
to annoy my brother's wife. I think
the fact that I manufacture door
knobs may have something to do with
it."

(Sutton & Cheam Herald)

A one-inch square of chocolate was
produced in court yesterday by a
policeman who alleged that a woman
had assaulted him with it.

(Birmingham Post)

The Chairman, Mr. K. N. Gambrill,
told Patterson: "You must not go
around putting your head through
other people's doors. It is a silly thing
to do."

(Sussex Express & County Herald)

*"You'll have to hurry the breakfast, sir,
it's time for your business lunch!"*

189

"I cannot write poems to order", says the new Poet Laureate. "I have to wait for the Muse."

Sorry you had to wait, Sir John; the Muse was round at Punch offices delivering this first batch.

NEW YEAR'S DAY 1973

Into Europe are we marching?
So the greyer papers say.
Common Market, Common People,
Commonness is here to stay.

Europe where in 1920
Drying on a salty shore
I found sand between my tootsies
And some flakes of apple core.

Europe seen from trike and hansom,
Metal palm trees *à la gare*.
In the bistro, marc, Dubonnet,
Scent of Gauloises or cigar.

Now my heart stays quietly homebound
Where the chill strikes through the choir.
Boiler-fumes enrich the incense,
Deathwatch beetles gnaw the spire.

Heath, who never sails to Europe,
Seems excited; I am cool.
Where abroad exists the equal
Of East Salford Ragged School?

ODE AT THE START OF THE OLYMPIC GAMES, 1976

Praise all the gymnasts at this great event,
    Including all the muscular viragoes,
All the competitors each country sent—
    Praise all the Comets and their stalwart cargoes!

Though that's a Cockney rhyme, I won't correct it:
    That is a habit I do not disown.
I trust the other lines to disinfect it.
    (I'm always doing that—they must have known.)

But praise (in any case) the bold contenders;
    Praise every candidate, however saurian;
Praise all of them, in their assorted genders!
    (If only they were gas-lit or Victorian . . .)

Let the tremendous contest now begin,
And may the least-to-blame performers win!

ON THE OPENING OF A NUCLEAR POWER STATION BY THE DUKE OF EDINBURGH

No clerestory, rood-tower, lectern or pew
    Embellishes anything here;
Every bit of this place you may pass in review
    Without finding one to revere.
It has to be secret—no Russians must know
The nuclear blessings our boffins bestow,
So even this poem's evasive, although
    Its actual aims are sincere.

How much more enjoyment church furnishings give
    Than nuclear power provides!
So many minutiae slip through the sieve
    Of anyone's longing. Besides,
Even though this establishment offers a wealth
Of atomic phenomena harmful to health,
It can still be at least beneficial by stealth:
    Still it is one of our prides.

THE PRINCE OF WALES'S MARRIAGE

O why are the Quality crowding the nave?
O why are the heralds so bright and so brave?
O why is the chancel as vivid as packs
Of aces and kings and of queens and of jacks?
Ochone! 'Tis the wedding of Charles, the young heir,
Whose charm has won hearts from Tralee to Kildare.

The Primate himself is to fasten the knot!
And divil the judge who would say he has not.
The organ swells out with a Mendelssohn theme,
While nobles and councillors glitter and gleam.
And outside the porch wait the crowds with their cheers,
Where Bridget and Paddy huzza all the peers.

There's hock in the narthex and game in the aisle,
And Princes and Sheiks and the Duke of Argyle.
The prime of the blood is on view in the fane,
With Pretenders to Portugal, Austria and Spain.
Huzza for the bridegroom! Bedad for the bride!
Good cess to the progeny they will provide!

Index of Artists

Index of Writers